SHOW

MW00904433

All Kinds of Love for All Kinds of Stories

Volume One – 2nd Edition

Pamela Jaye Smith

Monty Hayes McMillan

Published by MYTHWORKS
7231 Franklin Ave. Suite 5
Hollywood, CA 90046 USA
323-874-6447

pjs@pamelajayesmith.com
www.pamelajayesmith.com
www.mythworks.net
www.mythicchallenges.com
www.alphababeacademy.com

Manufactured in the United States of America

Cover art by Gail Jorden.

"Emotionally compelling, thoroughly enjoyable, full of insights for writers and non-writers alike. But absolutely essential for all writers. Love, or the lack of it, is at the heart of every story, no matter what the format. How clearly and profoundly that theme of love is expressed determines how well the story succeeds in touching an audience or reader. On a personal level, reading this book made me think deeply of the role of love in my personal life. And in my professional life, I will keep this as one of my most essential reference works."

Pam Wallace - Academy Award winning screenwriter, *Witness*

"This is a fantastic book! A joy to read, remarkable breadth and depth, with lots of humor! Pamela Jaye Smith is the world's foremost authority on mythology in screenwriting and filmmaking. Pamela and co-author Monty Hayes McMillan have crafted a perceptive and broad book on that most important topic – Love. Filled with examples, insights, and a deep understanding of the topic, this book will deepen your characters, story, themes, and visuals. A tremendous contribution to the art of storytelling."

Dr. Linda Seger – author, script consultant, international speaker www.lindaseger.com

"No matter what format you are working with -- film, television, novel, web series, play, etc. -- there is a strong likelihood that LOVE will be a large part of your storytelling foundation! *SHOW ME THE LOVE!* is a wonderful resource that defines the types of love and provides the invaluable tools to help you create the emotional core and motivation that will elevate your characters and their story!"

Kathie Fong Yoneda – international consultant and workshop leader
author *The Script-Selling Game* (2nd edition)
http://www.kathiefongyoneda.com

"*SHOW ME THE LOVE!* is witty, smart and fun...truly a comprehensive field manual to help you navigate the minefield of romance and all sorts of love. A must-have for both the lover and the lovelorn. And those who create the stories about them."
Geffrey von Gerlach, Life Coach and author of the novels *Ghostpoints, Beehive Arizona* and *Hexe: Witches, Warriors, Magic & Murder*

"This is a very well written, thought out guide. I am not an author nor do I have anything to do with the film industry. I am just an avid reader. This book has really opened my eyes on what the director or author is trying to visually accomplish in his or her film or book. I will definitely start paying more attention to symbols and camera angles in the future."
Deborah J. Richardson

"I would like to thank you very much for this **major work you have done** in making such a wonderful synthesis in SHOW ME THE LOVE. I love this way of writing, treating such complex aspects with a few sentences and words, getting to the heart while remaining very specific. That's really a signature of mastery!"
Alain Amouyal, Composer
www.amainamouyal.com

"I highly recommend this book to all writers, since most stories involve love in some form. Even non-writers will enjoy the detailed analysis of love in its many forms. The authors have provided a wonderful tool for us to spin our own unique tales by providing written descriptions, key elements, symbols, cinematic techniques and so much more for all of the various types of love. This enables writers to tap into the subliminal emotions that audiences experience, since mythological examples of love are highlighted throughout the book. There are loads of historical, film and television references made to amplify these points. I can't wait to collect the other books on love in this series!"
Jill Gurr, Founder and Exec Director - Create Now, produced screenwriter www.createnow.org

"Just finished your new tome of enlightenment last night...had a smile of satisfaction on my face, some very positive new ways to look at things. Very enjoyable and informative, you and Monty have definitely been doing your homework. I really like that you've given good, sharp, clear examples of the ideals/concepts for a writer and director/DP to use, among other creative folks. Your use of famous lines and images from movies really sell the point...as did camera angles."

>Steven A. Finly, WGAw   stevenfinly@sbcglobal.net
>*In Her Mother's Footsteps, Pressure Point, Wishful Thinking, Blackheart, Shadow Warriors*

"I just LOVE, SHOW ME THE LOVE!, which is a wonderful resource for everyone who is interested in "love," Filled with a plethora of references, examples, exercises and much more, this book is a terrific example of authors who love their subject. As a psychotherapist who deals with love, marriage, families, divorce--love gone bad and love that's great for over 30 years, I will be referring, "Show Me the Love!" not only to writers, but to individuals, couples and families who want to learn about all types of love, described and explained in this unique, and enlightening book."

>Dr. Rachel Ballon. Licensed Psychotherapist, International Writing Consultant, teacher and Author of 5 books on writing. http://www.rachelballon.com/

"SHOW ME THE LOVE! should be on the shelves of any serious writer. Without bogging us down in academic minutiae, SHOW ME THE LOVE! gives us ways to make our stories resonate with the elemental cultural underpinnings that make us human."

>Robert Grant – Writer/Producer-director RGO Media Associates   www.rgomedia.com
>Manager of Corporate Media, Hughes Aircraft Co.

DEDICATION

To those gone…

"For some we loved, the loveliest and the best
That from his Vintage rolling Time hath prest,
  Have drunk their Cup a Round or two before,
And one by one crept silently to Rest."
                    The Rubaiyat of Omar Khayyam

And those still here…

"For in and out, above, about, below,
'Tis nothing but a Magic-Shadow show,
  Play'd in a Box whose Candle is the Sun,
Round which we Phantom Figures come and go."
                    The Rubaiyat of Omar Khayyam

ACKNOWLEDGEMENTS

To all those writers, composers, poets, and artists in all media, the people whose passions create great art, great experience, and great inspiration.

Thanks to Aunt Betty and Uncle Fred Taylor for that sack of potatoes back when times were tougher than most people knew.

Many thanks to our inquisitive and creative readers and contributors: Dermot Davis, Brian Dyer, Judith Claire, Geffrey von Gerlach, Jill Gurr, Dave Kaplowitz, Reece Michaelson, Aurora Miller, Linda Seger, and Kathie Fong Yoneda.

Special thanks to Gail Jorden for the cover art, and to Tina Lewis for editing.

In 2000 Pamela Jaye first presented "What's Love Got To Do With It?" as one of a series of classes at the Philosophical Research Society in LA. Thanks for insights and information from my two guest speakers at that class, actress and screenwriter Victoria Foyt and filmmaker Lars Ulberg.

Pamela Jaye and Kathie Fong Yoneda co-taught a class at the Great American PitchFest on "What's Love Got To Do With It?" in 2010 which, along with an article they co-wrote for the GAP e-zine, helped inspire our own thinking on some of the various types of love.

Monty thanks – The University of Texas for teaching him to walk again, and for providing him with an education that led to a career in film.

Pamela, for "Seeing a talent I did not know I had". And to "My brother Jay, who has been very supportive of my career, though it has been the way of our family not to speak of such".

Special thanks to Mike Taylor and Larry Reibman for making the trip worthwhile.

Pamela thanks – Monty, for "getting me into film school and onto so many fabulous adventures, from the Arctic to the Andes to SE Asia. His unique and learned perspective on film, art, socio-politics, and travel has always made for fascinating conversations and experiences. Monty sees the vision, so often leads the way, and always has my back".

Special thanks to Rick Gilligan, Michael Wilson, Jim Bogart, Bruce Logan, Michael Ventura, and all the ladies of the Fun Patrol for decades of intriguing discussions about many aspects of Love.

Georgia Lambert, Wisdom Teacher, for lessons in the metaphysical aspects of all sorts of love.

TABLE OF CONTENTS

INTRODUCTION

SHOW ME THE LOVE! offers content creators of all genres, styles, and media a rich resource, new ideas, and a comprehensive, practical guide to using the dynamic and dramatic power of LOVE in all their stories.

Who is this book for? Writers, Directors, Actors, Directors of Photography, Production Designers, Composers, and Sound Designers as well as Development Execs, Producers, Publishers, and Marketers. Identifying, understanding, portraying, and communicating the core of emotion in a story is what entertains, enlightens, and educates your audience.

Understanding the deeper drives that affect how we act, react, and understand will give you better tools with which to create and motivate your characters and stories along their transformational arcs. Readers and viewers of all types of media may also find this information will enhance their understanding and enjoyment.

Our efforts to bring you a practical working knowledge of different types of love is not breaking new ground. We ride on the shoulders of others: Joseph Campbell, Robert Graves, Edith Hamilton, Norma Lorre Goodrich, Alfred Lord Tennyson, and many others. Much of the scientific material is thanks to researchers and reporters: Ethel Spector Person, Daniel G. Amen, Daniel J. Levitin, and publications such as Psychology Today, Science Daily, National Geographic, etc.

Most stories have some aspect of LOVE in them: romantic love, familial love, love of friends, love of self, love of country, love of the divine, love of animals, love of art, love of money, love of power, love of nature, love of death and destruction.

When well-crafted, the LOVE aspect of a story lives on in the hearts and minds of readers and viewers, be it "My old love! I'm paralyzed with happiness!" from *The Great Gatsby*; "I see you" from *Avatar*; "We few, we happy few, we Band of Brothers" from *Henry V*; *Casablanca*'s "We'll always have Paris"; "Greed is good", from *Wall Street*; "To boldly go where no one has gone before" from *Star Trek*; and from *Galaxy Quest*, the brilliant fun spoof of the *Star Trek* series, "As long as there is injustice, whenever a Targathian baby cries out, wherever a distress signal sounds among the stars, we'll be there. This fine ship, this fine crew. Never give up...and never surrender".

Some other languages pay more attention to nuances and have made a fine art of making a distinction between different variances in emotions and experiences. The Greeks have 16 words for various types love: Eros = sexual, Agape = reciprocal love between humans and the divine, Philios = familial, Patrios = love of country, Platonic = love without sex (as opposed to "Friends with Benefits"), etc.

The peoples of the Arctic regions have scores of words for snow and Swahili distinguishes eighteen grammatical genders. The word "love" is the basis for so many varied emotions but in English we only have the one word for all those very different things. Like English, Klingon has only one word for "love" and it is "bang", which kind of gets the meaning across on a number of levels.

The different types of LOVE can provide you with character and story arcs in any genre and any style, for instance:

LOVE of adventure is the plot driver of *Up* and *Star Trek*.

LOVE of or between deities can fuel epic stories such as *The Mahabharata*, the escapades of the Greco-Roman pantheon, the mythic characters in the *Ring Cycle* operas and *Lord of the Rings*.

LOVE of country is often the background for sagas such as *Out of Africa, Braveheart,* and *Avatar.*

Family stories often feature LOVE of animals, like *Tintin, Old Yeller, War Horse,* and *Free Willy;* as well as LOVE between animals, like *The Lion King, Lady and the Tramp, Finding Nemo,* and *Ice Age;* or between toys as in the *Toy Story* trilogy.

Buddy stories center on friendship's loyal LOVE such as Butch and Sundance, *Thelma and Louise,* and *The Hangover.*

LOVE of death and destruction motivates the antagonists The Joker in *The Dark Knight* and the Sith King in *Star Wars.*

Tragic stories often have twisted LOVE at their core, like *Phantom of the Opera, Quills, Eyes Wide Shut,* and *Deadwood.*

When romantic LOVE goes bad, it's all hell to pay, like in *The Girl, Fatal Attraction,* and *War of the Roses.*

Forbidden romantic LOVE can be quite tragic, as in *Anna Karenina* and *Brokeback Mountain.*

Bumbling romantic LOVE can be adorable and comedic like *When Harry Met Sally* and *The Wedding Crashers.*

Lost romantic LOVE offers sweet yearnings like in *Ghost, The Notebook,* and *Titanic.*

And there are many other types of LOVE that we will explore in this first book and in the ones to follow.

By knowing more about the psychological background of different types of love, by knowing how it has worked in myth, history, and current events, and by learning ways to express that type of love both in words and in visuals, you can make your stories richer and more memorable.

HOW TO USE THIS BOOK

SHOW ME THE LOVE! is a guidebook to many different types of love. It is a reference book for content creators to better craft the emotional situations and plot lines that will make your stories more compelling.

Using new technology doesn't automatically make you smarter; you still have to put in the brain-work. Conversely, if you don't have the latest equipment you can still appreciate and enjoy the media that you consume and/or create, on whatever level that may be.

Sometimes your story will present just a simple stroke of a certain type of love and that's just fine. Other times your story will explore the deeper complexities of your character's psyche, and having in-depth information will help you create richer back stories and subtext and give you inspiration for thoughts, dialogue, and actions.

We encourage you to write in this book. Add your own examples from movies, TV, books, comics, games, songs, history, current events, and your own life. Recognizing the pattern of a particular type of love will improve your ability to create that pattern in your own works.

Other volumes of the SHOW ME THE LOVE! series will follow, each with a selection of ten different kinds of love, such as *Gods and Goddesses in Love, Narcissism, Obsession, Star-Crossed Love, Sex for Sale, Superhero Love*, and many more.

*****

Following is the chapter format with a brief explanation of each category.

FORMAT

The Defining Myth
Myths are the stories we tell ourselves to explain, and often justify, the world around us and within us. Being able to draw upon an appropriate myth can greatly enrich your characters and your stories. Since love is the most fascinating emotion most people experience, it is the one most often turned into stories and immortalized in myths.

Exemplar Movie
Love is the precept for drama and drama is what motivates a story. "We'll always have Paris", "Frankly my dear, I don't give a damn", "We few, we happy few, we Band of Brothers", "Ooohhh, that's not right!" Some movies become iconic because of their use of love: how they reveal it, treat it, and hold it up as an example. The movies we list illustrate various kinds of love and how that type of love can move a story and improve a script. We use movies for examples since they are the most globally known and the easiest to access around the world.

Why this type of love exists – the evolutionary back-story
A lot of contemporary human behaviour is a heritage from our evolutionary past. Anthropologists point out that our hunter-gatherer history is reflected in some current relationships. Males, coming from a hunter background, are more prone to roam about and be always on the alert for new game, and ready to spread their seed to propagate the species. Females, coming from the gatherer background, are more prone to settle down in one spot to nurture the young children and focus their attention on keeping together the new family unit. And so it goes for many other of the drives and emotions that fall under the categories of "Love", be it love of land, of deities, of art, animals, etc.

How this type of love works – physiology and psychology
Hormones, chemicals, nerves, and psychological influences drive individuals to specific behaviours.

Testosterone and adrenaline drive young men to risky behaviour and to try to impregnate as many females as possible. Teenage girls are driven by estrogen and oxytocin to pair bond and reproduce. Both give off strong pheromones that can cause Romeo-and-Juliet situations, whether in 14th century Verona Italy or the local high school glee club.

In the category of patriotic love, for instance, young men are easily drafted into wars because they feel they are invincible. Older men with lowered testosterone levels are typically more mellow and more concerned for the group than for their own agendas. Women with higher testosterone levels often become warriors and leaders.

Psychological patterns from childhood can greatly influence a character's love-map, how they approach love and what they expect from it. Those early patterns can provide compelling scenes when the stress of the story brings on an emotional breakdown followed by a touching revelation of a character's core wound. ...except for the Joker in *Dark Knight*, who kept making up sad back stories for his own wickedness and then mocking those taken in by his so-called revelations.

These hormonal and psychological influences can be part of the back-story for your characters, how you define and reveal their nature.

How this type of love serves us now
Some evolutionary aspects still serve us well, such as the subtle signals of pheromones and other signs of physical health being indicators of a compatible immune system and reproductive fitness. Other evolutionary aspects are about gaining and protecting resources, which can explain the deep roots of greed, hoarding, and gossip (a social monitoring and control system for keeping people in line). Artists, rebels, and misfits are seldom bound by any of the ancient social drives and can choose their attractions based on talent, glamour, eccentricity, and the ability to inspire.

The explanation matters because the more you know about how it got to be this way, the richer your characters and story can be.

Examples in Myth and Legend
Some of the greatest stories ever told have been told and retold for aeons. Most of the stories we currently tell each other are just updates and variations of the timeless classics. And that's okay. Just as children want to hear over and over and over again the same stories, so too do grownups; but we want some novelty tossed in as well.

That's your job as content creators, to embrace the core principles of a theme, archetype, situation, symbol, etc. but to present it in a new way so that we can learn the lessons anew, enjoy again that thrill of discovery, and be satisfied with how it all turns out.

Examples in History and Current Events
Your story can gain legitimacy and/or immediacy if you have appropriate references to actual past and/or present events. It's also good research for you to make your story arcs and character arcs more realistic – even in fantasy genres.

Some production companies and networks specifically search for stories that address contemporary issues even if they are period pieces. Because history so often repeats itself, knowing what went before can give you an advantage in crafting your story.

Examples in Media
Watch and read other media dealing with your chosen concept of love to learn what has been done, what works, and what does not. After having done that research, you will be inspired to use the relevant basics and to put your own unique twist on that type of love.

Examples in Music
Different styles of music affect us in different ways -- martial music, sorrowful music, celebratory music, spiritual music, romantic music, etc.

Sound deeply affects us both physiologically and psychologically. Though it is not a visual art, for some people who have synasthesia, sound actually creates visuals and emotions in their brains. For the rest of us, it stirs our imaginations. Dvorak's New World Symphony [No. 9 in E minor] creates the images of a thunderstorm rolling across the countryside.

Some of these examples may give you ideas for your soundtrack, or for references within your novel.

Symbols
In our multicultural, instantaneously interconnected global village, we speak hundreds of languages and thousands of dialects with diverse and specific cultural backgrounds. How can we communicate effectively across all these borders?

Symbols and images convey emotions, states of mind, and actions frozen in time. Bernini's exquisite marble statue of Saint Teresa of Avila quivers with the ecstasy of adoration. A flower crushed in bloody battlefield mud captures war's tragic futility. A raised fist commemorates a revolution, a raised flag a victory, and a bird rising in flight a valiant act or a release to freedom.

Visuals are a universal language that engage our intuition and imagination.

Key Element – the Shining Moment
You must have that one defining moment around which everything else pivots. It is purity, clarity. It is the image on the movie poster, the book cover, on YouTube thumbnail. It is the bumper sticker quote.

Is it dialogue or action? It can be either or both and it can be truly just a moment or it can last an entire scene sequence. Sometimes it's the long-awaited kiss, sometimes it's jumping in front of someone to take the bullet.

In *Armageddon*, the guys draw straws to see who'll stay behind on the asteroid and trigger the nuke that will blow it to smithereens and save Earth. Bruce Willis's Harry Stamper sabotages the guy who drew the short straw, pushes him into the spaceship, slams the door, and takes on the responsibility of blowing the nuke. He's sacrificing his own life to save all of humanity – that is the Shining Moment.

Written Descriptions

In prose you are the director, art director, costumer, makeup artist, and acting coach for every aspect of the story. Sure, you leave some things for the readers' imagination or your story won't engage their imagination, but they want you to create and evoke a rich world for them to explore.

For scripts to be sold and turned into a visual medium, you must first impress a development exec or reader with words on a page. Scripts suggest to the director, production designer, cinematographer, lighting director, costumer, and actors what you envision, so they can use that as a springboard for their own interpretations and creativity.

You want to use adverbs, adjectives, verbs, and nouns that liven up the page. E.g. instead of "walk", you could use plods, scurries, prances, etc. Instead of "eats" you could use picks at, devours, gulps, or for a classier approach, dines. Give inanimate objects human characteristics such as "leaves shivering in the wind".

Make your pages more powerful by using potent, visceral words that engage our imagination and our love of story.

Cinematic Techniques
This section has suggestions on framing, composition, lighting, sound, music, and so on, to create the effect you're after, particularly for those Shining Moments that SHOW ME THE LOVE!

Conclusion

Exercises in Awareness & Writing
Now put to use what you have learned in each chapter using these brief exercises.

Further Reading

Further Viewing/Media

CHAPTER ONE

LOVE OF LAND & COUNTRY

This land is your land, this land is my land....

"This Land is Your Land"
Woody Guthrie

One of the most basic loves people have is a love of their homeland. By bringing out this aspect you can deepen your characters and give them even more to care about, fear to lose, fight and even die for. These stakes are high and unmistakable. It can be an effective reflection about how they feel about other characters – either by comparison or contrast.

After gender identification what we notice most or most want to know about others is their ethnic origin which may tell us something about their patriotic allegiance. Sometimes this seems evident by the colour of their skin and/or their speech. The assumption is that people will carry the imprint of their homeland and will act in certain ways depending on where they are from.

On a planet increasingly stressed by both natural and manmade changes, love of the very land itself may be the essential key to alleviating the ongoing damage and bringing Earth back into balance with itself and every life form on it and in it.

The Defining Myth
The Garden of Eden, that idyllic land where there was no sickness, want, or death. And where the land itself was used to create humanity – man made from the dust of the very earth.

Most cultures look back with yearning to some Golden Age when they were living in a better place and everything was better, from the weather to the crops to the neighbors (or the lack thereof). This idealization of the actual physical earth as the source of all that was well before and which could be well again engages some driven and sometimes desperate part of the human psyche that imagines and desires perfection.

Exemplar Movie
Out of Africa, "I had a farm in Africa."

Why it exists (evolutionary back-story)
Love of the land is a basic instinctual reverence for that which supports one's very existence. The physical land supplies the resources necessary for sheer survival and at some level we just know that, or we used to anyway, back when everyone knew where their food came from. These days, maybe not so much because love of your local grocery store just isn't quite the same as love of the fertile land.

The desert Fremen of *Dune* loved and respected their land and though to everyone else it was a bleak forbidding wasteland, they learned to thrive on it. The Fremen were patterned after the nomadic Bedouin of Arabia and North Africa.

How it works (physiology & psychology)
We have a specific, direct connection to the land because it is what we are made of. The land is in our bones and in our teeth, as well as our hearts. As is often a plot point in scientifically-slanted procedural dramas, deductions about a victim can be made from spectro-analysis of the various minerals and other markers in their bodies.

How it serves us now

Ecologically speaking, the developed world seems to have lost touch with this basic love of the land. We are refusing to admit that there may be troubles in paradise. We are misusing and abusing the planet and the evidence of that is all around us. Mother Nature ultimately wins so it seems like it would behoove us to be on her side.

Like kids on a playground in an endless game of "King of the Mountain", peoples keep shouldering each other off the land, usually with force of arms backed up by provable or sometimes specious historical or theological claims.

A character engaged with ecology can not only be an integral part of your story but can also make a point about your personal perspective on the planet, resources, etc. The current trend of apocalyptic stories are set against a damaged environment.

Examples in Myth and Legend

The Wandering Jew and the Flying Dutchman were both cursed to wander homelessly.

Moses and the Israelites searched forty years for the Promised Land.

The Hopi myths tell of their wanderings up, down, and across the North and South American continents in search of their perfect homeland.

Examples in History and Current Events

Ecology and the environment motivate many people. "Tree-huggers", deep ecologists, and land rights organizations stand up to rampant and often destructive development. Examples are the Environmental Protection Agency, the Endangered Species Act, various Native American groups, Greenpeace, and others. Documentaries often address these issues, such as *The Cove* about dolphin hunting in Japan, Al Gore's movie *Inconvenient Truths*, and *Silent Water*.

Naturalists are people who not only love nature but love to be out in it, as do Stephen Maturin in the *Master and Commander* series, Grizzly Adams, and Jeremiah Johnson. The Australian Aborigines have a phenomenally close connection with the land. Both *The Last Wave* and *Australia* are films that explore their love of the land.

Survivalists are people who resort to nature as a rejection or fear of civilization. They have learned to live in the absence of civilization, often in a post-apocalyptic world such as in *Waterworld, The Postman, Road Warrior, Tank Girl, The Road* and the reality TV series *Doomsday Preppers*.

Conquerors measure their success by the amount of land they control as did Genghis Khan, Attila the Hun, the Mogul invasion of India, Alexander the Great, the Roman Empire, the British Empire, and the Conquistadores. *The Mission* shows how that worked in South America. The Great Wall of China was built to keep out invaders from Mongolia.

Examples in Media
Lawrence of Arabia's T.E. Lawrence - "Englishmen like the desert because it's so… clean." Anthony Quinn - "You British dream of the desert. Us Bedouins dream of green fields and fountains."

The French family in *Apocalypse Now Redux* is so tied to the land that they do not evacuate their plantation even as the Vietnam war ramps up, but maintain their colonial lifestyle in the midst of that dangerous conflict.

In Bram Stoker's *Dracula*, the Count travels with dirt from the homeland in his coffin. In *Saving Private Ryan* one of the soldiers collects soil samples from every place they have invaded.

In *Gone with the Wind* Scarlet O'Hara's father tells her, "Land, Scarlet, land". Towards the end she lifts a handful of the red dirt of Tara and swears never to be hungry again.

The humans in *Battlestar Galactica* were searching for their homeland -- Earth.

Lost Horizon portrays a very special relationship between land and people. There, the humans have held back Nature's trek of time, as long as they stay in the Himalayan retreat of Shangri-La. But if they step off that special territory, time catches up with them in a dramatic way as they quickly fast-forward to what should be their normal age.

Field of Dreams is about baseball and not the environment, but this magical piece of land is so powerful on so many levels that it has become a shrine for baseball fans around the world. Some even buy samples of the dirt to take back take home.

And of course, *Avatar* is about the Na'vi's connection to their land. The antagonists want parts of that land in a calculated military-backed imposition of extraction capitalism. The hero changes sides and helps them save their land, thus winning the heart of his true love.

Examples in Music
"America the Beautiful"
"Anthem" – Josh Groban
"The Hebrides" aka *Fingal's Cave Overture* – Felix Mendelssohn
"Oklahoma!"
"New World Symphony" - Dvorak
"This Land is Your Land" – Woody Guthrie
"Woodstock" – Joni Mitchell
"Till the Last Shot's Fired" – Trace Adkins
http://www.dardensmith.com/projects/songwriting-with-soldiers-history/

Symbols
The dirt itself. The fertile soil of Tara in *Gone with the Wind* or the devastated Midwest plains in *Grapes of Wrath*.

Wide expanses of the landscape. Mountains. Vast plains. Mines. Amber waves of grain. Jungles.

A rock, pebble, plant.

Crystals.

Key Element – the Shining Moment
Kissing the earth.

Carrying the homeland soil with them.

Returning to home from far, far away.

Planting their feet on the ground again. Maybe even barefoot.

Gazing with love and awe across the landscape.

Written Descriptions
Elaborate. Spell it out. Don't just have you character say, "I love Texas". Have them say something about the great plains being the bottom of the Permian Ocean and that "I just cruised across the bottom of a long-gone ancient ocean and saw creatures beyond my imagination".

"I love LA" by Randy Newman. Listen to his lyrics about why he loves Los Angeles.

Karen Blixen's *Letters from Africa* is a book about her many years out there on a coffee farm. Her real name is Isak Dinesen and her life inspired the book and the film OUT OF AFRICA.

"Not enough understanding exists regarding land and it's place in the Irish soul. There's a primitive feeling for acreage on this island; there always was, there always will be. A man will still kill for a field more than he'll kill for money, revenge, or a woman....After all, in some of our earliest and wildest mythologies, our gods mated with the earth, and our ancestors chose to lie in the earth after they died." p.566 *Ireland* – Frank Delaney

Anthropomorphize the land – Mother Earth, the Fatherland, the rolling hills like a woman's curves.

Cinematic Techniques
Shooting "on the deck" (on the ground) conveys a close connection between your character and the land or it can convey the character of the land itself. Dry barren earth, rows of plowed furrows, sprouting plants, small animal holes, the spongy carpet in a three-canopy jungle, crunching snow, etc.

Environmental shot: wide angle, hold it a long time, let the land speak for itself, fuse the viewer into the land, allow your audience enough time to absorb the entire environment. Director David Lean was very good at that, particularly in *Lawrence of Arabia* and *Ryan's Daughter*. Writer-director Terence Malick in *Days of Heaven* and *The Thin Red Line* made the land itself a large part of the story.

Just the opposite of this is the film *Koyaanisqatsi,* in which the camera was locked down with an attached inter-velometer recording single frames over a long period of time. The result is a continuous series of speeded-up time-lapse photography which imparts a sense of longer geological time.

Sweeping aerial shot: moves along the land in a visual caress. *Out of Africa, The English Patient, The Lord of the Rings* trilogy, *Wings* (the first film to win an Academy Award for Best Picture), and *Battle of Britain*. The 1971 Oscar-winning documentary *Sentinels of Silence* features a stunning 18-minute helicopter ride over the ruins and landscape of the pre-Columbian Mayan empire. The Mexican government still shows this film in their embassies around the world.

Conclusion

Because it is such an integral part of being human, bringing this love of land into your characters makes them more sympathetic and identifiable. Millions of people have fought and died over claims of ownership and the "right of return", from Genghis Khan to the Conquistadors, from the Vikings to the Ainu, from the Boer Wars to Zionist claims in Palestine. There is a very rich well of history and current events from which to pull dramatic conflict in this type of love.

*****

Exercise #1 – Awareness

Answer these questions for one of your characters. Do you live now where you were born? What do you think of when you think of your place of origin? Does it draw you or repel you? What is the worst thing that could happen to your land? What would you be willing to do to protect your homeland?

*****

Exercise #2 – Writing

Write some dialogue where one character is explaining their love of the land to another character who just doesn't get it. E.g. a fifth-generation rancher to a big-city girl.

*****

Further Reading

Dune - Frank Herbert
Gone with the Wind – Margaret Mitchell
Ireland - Frank Delaney
James Michener: *Hawaii, Centennial, Alaska, Texas*, etc.
Mars Trilogy - Kim Stanley Robinson
Memories and Visions of Paradise: ...Myth of a Lost Golden Age – Richard Heinberg
Outlander – Diana Gabaldon
Silent Spring – Rachel Carson
The Thorn Birds – Colleen McCullough

Further Viewing

20,000 Leagues Under the Sea
Australia
An Inconvenient Truth
Battlestar Galactica
Blood Diamonds
Burden of Dreams
Days of Heaven
Deep Blue
Emerald Forest
Enemy at the Gates
Far and Away
Fitzcarraldo
Giant
Grapes of Wrath, The
Green Acres
Iwo Jima
Koyaanisqatsi
McCleod's Daughters
Munich
Oklahoma!
Places in the Heart
Road Warrior
The Field
Thin Red Line
Thornbirds
Wall-E
Warriors
Waterworld
Woodstock

Silent Water documentary
Mythic Challenges
WATER www.onedrop.org
Love Calling: Writing Songs with Soldiers
http://www.dardensmith.com/projects/songwriting-with-soldiers-history/

CHAPTER TWO

FAMILIAL LOVE

"Remember this, all of you. Nothing counts so much as blood.
The rest are just strangers."

Wyatt Earp
Nicholas Earp

The old saying goes, "Blood is thicker than water", meaning
that family connections are stronger than any other
ties....supposedly. Though it's a holdover from our herd, pack,
and tribal past, it's still very much in play today.

Unlike love for a large impersonal thing like land, this type of
love is very personal and specific between individuals. It can
also engage groups such as family units, tribes, and some
religious and fraternal orders.

Family sagas are so engaging because unless we were left in
a basket on the church steps most of us have family of some
sort that comforts us, drives us mad, inspires us, discourages
us...and sometimes all of the above.

Family dynamics are so dramatic that most adult therapy
clients deal with the leftovers from childhood and most young
therapy clients are dealing with the current effects of the family
units.

Family tragedies mark everyone they touch, usually in very
disruptive ways. Modern stories reflecting that are *Ordinary
People, The Descendants*, the TV series *Revenge,* and that
international hit, *Dallas.*

Some family situations are so stereotypical you just need one phrase to conjure up an entire palette of behaviours and emotions: mother-in-law, stepfather, kissing cousins, you're like a brother to me, sugar daddy, momma's boy, daddy's little princess, and that poor red-headed stepchild.

In this category we focus on stories where the family relationships drive the plot and the character arcs, rather than stories that just have families in them as character background, etc.

The Defining Myths
King Agamemnon sacrificed his virgin daughter Iphigenia to get the winds to sail the Greek fleet to Troy and begin the Trojan War. Upon his return ten years later his still angry and grieving wife Clytemnestra murdered him with the help of her ambitious lover, who coincidentally was not a good stepfather to the remaining children.

Wagner's *Ring Cycle* operas have all sorts of family dynamics going on among the Teutonic gods, mortal, demi-gods, dwarves, giants and sea nymph sisters, a lot of it rather troublesome and tragic but set to quite stirring music.

Exemplar Movies
On Golden Pond and *The Descendants*

Why it exists (evolutionary back-story)
Family units are a genetic insurance policy. The members collaborate, look out for each other, and help ensure the survive-and-thrive of their unique family gene pool.

The wicked stepmother is a staple in fairy tales. Some say this genetic cleansing followed by re-booting the gene pool explains why step-parents are often so cruel to the step-children – it's instinctual. You see it in animals, such as when a new tomcat kills the other tomcat's kittens, breeds with all the female cats and starts a new gene pool.

This execution of an entire family line happened a lot in ancient times in many royal bloodline situations. Regicide, infanticide, fratricide, etc. are so common as to be the unremarkable in the history books. Read or watch *I, Claudius* for some bloody dramatic examples of this concept of purifying or wiping out a bloodline.

Filial piety is a moral construct meant to ensure that the multiple generations of a family support each other. Ancestor worship is a part of this system. Many feared the one-child policy of China would undermine the system and old people would be left to fend for themselves. We still have not seen the final results of this societal shift.

How it works (physiology & psychology)
Genealogy is the emotional attachment to heritage, a search for personal identity and a sense of belonging, and if you're lucky, the importance of your ancestors. Everyone looks for that lost duke but many find horse thieves instead.

Siblings can be a mirroring device leading to self-knowledge: you can quite clearly see what you want and do not want to be. Some parents try to live their own unfulfilled dreams through their children; typically this does not go well. Two extravagant examples are Mama Rose in *Gypsy* and Joan Crawford in *Mommie Dearest*.

Families have a shared history of experience that others simply cannot understand. There are special languages and stories that when retold at family gatherings strengthen the familial emotional bonds.

In *True Lies* and *The Last Boy Scout* you have dysfunctional daughters who don't like their fathers. Both dads live a lie: Arnold Schwarzenegger as a secret agent and Bruce Willis as a detective. In *Contact*, Jodie Foster's dad was very supportive of her celestial ambitions.

The mother-son relationship in *The Grifters* is particularly twisted by crime and incest. In *Sons and Lovers* the emotionally possessive mother-son relationship hinders the young man's ability to have a healthy love relationship with a girl his own age.

Many stories are about finding the father and/or winning the father's love. E.g. *Thor, Indiana Jones*, and *The Great Santini*. The complex family dynamics of Luke Skywalker, his sister Princess Leia, and their father Darth Vader are foundational plot points for the entire *Star Wars* series. The wonderful *Young Indiana Jones* TV series has a through-line of Indy's remote father not being able to express his love.

How it serves us now
Even in this fractured world of global interconnections, families split by work, diverse interests, distracting media, and new family ties, there is something about that core family that still exerts a pull.

Think of all the drama around holiday family gatherings - weddings, births, funerals...all are ripe fodder for your stories.

A family's support or lack thereof can create tight situations for your heroine. In many cultures there is still the expectation that elderly parents will be cared for by the unmarried daughter, the eldest son and his family, the gay son, etc. And yet, most Americans place their elders in "assisted living" homes.

Just as we learn a lot from watching our friends around their families, you the writer can reveal a lot about a character by showing us her family, either directly or via her back-story.

Examples in Myth and Legend
The Atriedes clan in Greek mythology took family loyalty to cannibalistic extremes.

Another Greek myth tells about Medea, who when spurned by her husband Jason for a younger local princess killed the interloper, killed her own two sons by Jason, and fled the country.

In the Arthurian legends, Morgaine is King Arthur's half-sister and she seduces him in some versions. In Marion Zimmer Bradley's *Mists of Avalon*, she is tasked as a child to "take care of" her little brother, Arthur. Their mating is part of a seasonal pagan ritual, rather than a calculated seduction.

Examples in History and Current Events
Dynasties from the ancient Egyptian to the Chinese, the Roman Empire, and the ruling families of Europe are complex inter-woven webs of family blood, loyalties, and rivalries.

A number of ancient societies married brother and sister to keep the blood line pure. Many feudal systems practiced *le droit seigneur* where the lord of the land deflowers every bride, fathering a lot of children and keeping that genetic connection active within his fiefdom. That was a major emotional event in *Braveheart*.

In modern times there are still ruling families in business [Rupert Murdoch's, the Coors family], in show biz [Fondas, Clooneys, Danner/Paltrow], the Kardashians] and in politics [the Kennedys, the Bushes].

And in the adventure side of show biz you have the Flying Walendas, and Evel Knievel and his son Robbie.

Communes of the American Hippie era attempted to create a lateral family from non-related people with no structural hierarchy. Vertical families are the typical grandma, granddad, mom, dad, kids, etc. The retired spies in RED were a lateral family.

A high divorce rate and more non-married moms has created a lot of single-parent families and blended families. The lack of the large support structure of an extended family is often thought to be detrimental.

Running vendettas sometimes pit family members against each other, sometimes it's family against family, as in the Hatfields and the McCoys, and the Taylors and Suttons.

Examples in Media
Game of Thrones is rich with family intrigue, loyalties, and betrayals that drive the plot of the stories. Same with *The Borgias*.

Love Actually has many different types of familial relationships in varying states of strength or disarray.

Frank Herbert's *Dune* series of novels contains feudal houses patterned after those of Medieval and Renaissance Europe.

Sibling rivalry drives many people and many stories: *East of Eden*, the Danish film *Brothers*, *A River Runs Through It*, *The Other Boleyn Girl*, and *Twins*. A fun example of sibling loyalty is *Boondock Saints*.

In *Quigley Down Under* Laura san Giocomo plays a mother who has accidentally smothered her child trying to keep it quiet during an Indian attack. It drives her over the edge of madness with grief and remorse. *Sophie's Choice* is a different setup but is steeped in the guilt over a child's death.

In *Peter Pan* there are three family clusters: the Darlings, Peter and the Lost Boys with Wendy as mom and Peter as Dad, and the Pirates.

In the *Harry Potter* stories the Dursleys are a wretched family Harry is happy to escape. The Weasely family is his ideal and he spends lots of time with Ron, Ginnie, the twins, and their parents.

Boogie Nights isn't really about the porn industry, it is about creating a lateral family.

The Royal Tenenbaums is about an eccentric father who wants to make things right with his three grown children, who are all prodigies of some kind, and their mother.

In TV we've had *The Brady Bunch, The Partridge Family, The Bill Cosby Show, All in the Family, Malcolm in the Middle, Bonanza, Married with Children, Fresh Prince of Bel Air..* Mid-century American TV programming suggested an ideal of what the American family should have been like in *Father Knows Best, Leave it to Beaver, Ozzie and Harriet, The Danny Thomas Show, The Donna Reed Show.* In the mid-late 60s it became painfully apparent this ideal was definitely not real.

This absurdity peaked with *The Partridge Family* and then came *All in the Family,* in which Norman Lear was able to make socio-political statements about family and society couched in an irreverent comedy series.

And who can ever forget those first nighttime soaps from the 80s, *Dallas* and *Dynas*ty.

Dysfunctional families fill the airwaves these days with *The Simpsons* (the longest running TV show in America), *Arrested Development, Modern Family, Two and a Half Men, Numbers, Fringe,* and many more.

Water for Chocolate is an example of someone fighting the demands of filial piety.

Examples in Music
"Chicken Fried" - Zac Brown Band
"In Color" - Jamey Johnson
"If Heaven Wasn't So Far Away" - Justin Moore
"Together" from *Gypsy*
 "We are Family" – Sly and the Family Stone

The Jackson Five, Hanson Brothers, Jonas Brothers, and the Lennon Sisters.

Symbols
Some birthmark or heraldry item. In *Game of Thrones* there is the dragon symbol.

The identity of the "hidden baby" in many stories is revealed by a physical feature such as nose, hair or eye colour. *The Importance of Being Earnest* is a charming story woven around this hidden baby plot.

Knots. Trees. Interlocking hands. Blood.

Key Element – the Shining Moment
Fierce loyalty -- as when in the latest incarnation *Star Trek* film young Spock fights the other young Vulcan boys because they dissed his mom.

The rescue. Sometimes the young ones save elders like in *Spy Kids*; sometimes it's vice versa.

The embrace of reconciliation.

The welcoming celebration ala the Prodigal Son *Bible* story.

Written Descriptions
Show a sense of both similarity and differences. "Tall like his brother, he was broader in the shoulders."

Have two or more characters do the same thing, say the same phrase, something to denote their mutual background. In *The Italian Job* when bad guy Ed Norton realizes Charlize Theron is Donald Sutherland's daughter when she repeats one of his catch-phrases.

In *Wyatt Earp* starring Kevin Costner the father Nicholas [Gene Hackman] says to his boys, "Remember this, all of you. Nothing counts so much as blood. The rest are just strangers."

In British crime shows there is often an undiscovered brother or sister working at back angles to the main story, providing dramatic plot twists in the end when all is revealed. Good examples are the *Hercule Poirot* mysteries, *The Importance of Being Earnest,* and the *Mrs. Bradley* mysteries.

In Romance novels the "secret baby" is a popular trope.

Other ways to convey familial relationships include birthmarks, eye colour, accents, or other physical traits like in *The Coneheads* – it's real obvious they're related.

Cinematic Techniques
In multiple family-member situations instead of camera angles use wardrobe and props to differentiate each distinct sibling.

In blocking, put the predominant sibling in the foreground, or looming large in the background.

Since this concept is about people of the same flesh, show hands (or other body parts such as arms, heads, lips) touching or going apart.

Between adult and child is a downward angle to show the hierarchy, power and protection or unfortunately sometimes, power and suppression or abuse. Between siblings the angles are more face to face, and between adults it's more face to face.

Be very specific with your angles to get across the point of who has the power and how they are using it. Use an upward angle to show sinister intent; a downward angle to reveal innocence. Thought they are not about family in particular some exaggerated examples of this technique are *The Cabinet of Dr. Caligari* http://www.imdb.com/media/rm205953024/tt0010323 for an example of the former and the old silent movie series *The Perils of Pauline* for the latter. http://en.wikipedia.org/wiki/The_Perils_of_Pauline_(1914_seri al)

Conclusion
No matter your story's genre, style, setting, or main plot you can enrich your characters and add dramatic tension by including some family dynamics, whether with the presence of the actual related people or by reference to them through conversation, photos, etc.

Family sagas are always popular and offer you lots of great opportunities to explore various versions of and intensities of Familial Love.

In your writing, give us a sense of similarities and differences. "Though decades apart in age, that smile was so similar as to remove any doubt about their shared heritage."

Keep in mind that families make us who we are, whether they are present or not. Genetics, psychology, philosophies all influence us in varying ways at various ages. By including some family dynamics in your stories you will give your audiences much richer and more memorable characters.

*****

Exercise #1 – Awareness
What is the most dramatic example of familial love or hate you can think of, from myth, media, or actual life?

*****

Exercise #2 – Writing
Write or select a scene of at least three exchanges of dialogue where two people are not related.

Then write the same scene with the two people related in some way: parents, siblings, cousins.

*****
Further Reading
The Genesis account of Cain and Abel
The Bible account of Joseph and his brothers selling him into slavery
A River Runs Through It – Norman Maclean
Bastard out of Carolina – Dorothy Allison
East of Eden – John Steinbeck
Forsyte Saga, The – John Galsworthy
Joy Luck Club, The – Amy Tan
To Kill a Mockingbird – Harper Lee

Further Viewing
Adams Family, The   *Auntie Mame*
Big Fish, The
Birdcage / La Cage au Folle
Boogie Nights
Brady Bunch, The – TV series
Cat on a Hot Tin Roof   *Christmas Story, The*
Chronicles of Narnia   *Dallas* – TV series
Departed, The   *Fringe* – TV series
Gypsy   *Home Alone*
Incredibles, The   *Juno*
Kids are All Right, The   *Little Miss Sunshine*
National Lampoon's Family Vacation
Numbers – TV series   *Revenge* – TV series
Sons of Katie Elder   *Sophie's Choice*
Sound of Music, The   *Stepfather*
Swiss Family Robinson   *Terms of Endearment*
Tree of Life
Two and a Half Men – TV series
Wyatt Earp   *Yours, Mine, and Ours*

CHAPTER THREE

BFF = Best Friends Forever

I love you, You love me,
We're best friends like friends should be.

Sung by Barney the purple dinosaur
words and music by Elmer Bernstein

A True Friend...

Scolds like a dad.
Cares like a mom.
Teases like a sister.
Irritates like a brother.

Platonic love can be defined as a closeness, an affinity,
loyalty, and enjoyment of the other person with no tinge of the
erotic from either party.

This kind of love can be primary or a very important secondary
part of your plot.

Regardless of whether or not the people see each other a lot or just every once in awhile, once that bond is made it holds true in spite of the years, political views, relatives, etc. You can call them up after twenty years and the bond is still there. When you see each other after a long time apart, it's like you were just together yesterday and you pick up right where you left off.

The Protagonist can have friends, sure. But unless that friendship itself is integral to the plot or to that character's development, it doesn't qualify as a BFF story.

Greek philosopher Aristotle observed that friendship is essential to human thriving. He noted that it comes in three versions:

1) those based on utility such as Facebook, LinkedIn, and other business and social contacts

2) those based on pleasure such as dancing or drinking, museums, book and movie buddies

3) those based on a shared pursuit of virtue — this often falls into the categories of religions and philosophy.

Aristotle believed that real friends are attracted to the best within each other. They are supportive, even when the friend makes mistakes or does not live up to their potential.

The BFF helps you become who you really are. Friendship, like love, depends on idealization. Although the BFF is supposed to be always loyal, dramatic conflict can arise when friends do something we disapprove of or do not understand. That can put the friendship on hold or end it entirely. In *The Four Feathers* when one young soldier admits, "I don't want to go to war", it affects the friendships of the other three soldiers and his girlfriend. Then when he saves their lives and returns the white feathers – which are symbolic of cowardice -- they are all friends once again as he has redeemed himself and taken his place in the ideology of the friendships.

Some people are so desperate for friendship they overlay their desires on an unsuspecting or unworthy person. There's an adorable greeting card with a picture of a little boy lying on the grass petting his turtle. He gazes at it affectionately and the word bubble says, "You're my best friend". The thought bubble above the turtle says, "You're pathetic". An example of the unworthy or dangerous projection of BFF is *The Talented Mr. Ripley.*

The Defining Myth
The Mesopotamian story of arrogant, sophisticated, womanizing king Gilgamesh and Enkidu, the gentle naive animal-loving man of the wilderness is one of the oldest "buddy stories". It pits the city against the countryside, the vain against the humble, worldly versus innocent, the outgoing versus the introvert. Through the course of the story as they first fight and then struggle to work together, they bond into a true friendship that battles petty gods, scorned goddesses, scorpion men, fickle fate, helpful strangers and the ultimate tragedy of separation by death.

Exemplar Movies
Butch Cassidy and the Sundance Kid, Thelma and Louise, Lawrence of Arabia, Tropic Thunder

Why it exists (evolutionary back-story)
Cooperation helps the survival of the group. Early man hunting in pairs won more battles with mammoths. In hunter-gatherer groups working together is essential.

"Who can you trust?" is a vital question for all of us. In your stories this is the purpose of the Sidekick, the Best Friend. They are the person who helps the Heroine, is loyal to her, is a sounding board for her – that is their function.

Reciprocity. The expectation of payback is certainly a part of the motivation behind taking care of our friends. The opportunity for dramatic conflict lies in a character's failure to stand by their friend..."After all I've done for you!?"

How it works (physiology & psychology)
There are mirror neurons in our brains that control the monkey-see monkey-do phenomenon. Note how when you're interacting with someone you will both reach up to scratch your head at the same time, or twist your hands together, or... Our brains are wired to reflect each other.

We are also wired for friendship and altruism.
http://www.sciencedaily.com/releases/2013/08/1308220858
04.htm

There are three categories of cues for friendship: proximity, affinity, commonality.

Proximity – when you're younger it's who is in your immediate environment of school and playground. When older it can be college, work, prison, the armed forces, office cubicles, etc. *Jumping Jack Flash, 9 to 5, Office Space, Glengarry Glen Ross, Alien(s), Upstairs Downstairs*

Affinity – Sports, playing cards, video games, car clubs, opera, movies. It's not the organization, it's the people in it. Trekkies – *Free Enterprise.* Bowling – *The Big Lebowski.* Surfing - *Point Break.* And of course, the guys in the *Hangover* series.

Commonality – Some BFFs are tied by some commonality. Divorce in *The Odd Couple.* Thelma and Louise are both tired of life. *The Banger Sisters* share memories of being rock-and-roll groupies. There could also be a 12-step program, where there's the commonality of addiction.

You also see the opposite of this in *The Odd Couple*, where Oscar and Felix don't have any affinity for each other, but they do have commonality. The story is about their lack of affinity which creates the tension between the characters and allows the story arc to continue.

Observe all three together – proximity, affinity, commonality -- in real life on film sets and in theatre groups, such as the Canadian TV series *Slings and Arrows.*

How it serves us now

We can all appreciate the comfort of a close friendship. As a subset of the larger community, it helps create and draw the community closer together on an individual level that affects the larger group. What Homer Simpson does with his neighbor Ned helps the larger community of Springfield. That relationship is part of the bigger community. The rewards from a deep and lasting friendship are both personal and for the group.

Best Friends can inspire us to be the best we can be. The best ones hold that image of our potential in focus and keep it safe for us, regardless of what we do. The best ones believe in us, at the highest level.

Examples in Myth and Legend

Hercules and Aeolus in Greek myth. Robin Hood, Friar Tuck, and Little John in English folklore. Gunnar and Siegfried in Teutonic myths immortalized in *Gotterdammerung*, the fourth of the Ring Cycle operas.

Examples in History and Current Events

Stanley and Livingston, British explorers in Africa.
Sir Edmund Hilary, the first person to successfully climb Mt. Everest, and Tengsin Norgay, his Sherpa guide.
Apollo and Space Shuttle mission crews.
And think about your own Best Friends from grade school, high school, college, work, life. You'll probably find some emotions and actions there that can inspire incidents that will ring true in your stories.

Examples in Media

Butch Cassidy and the Sundance Kid
Captain Richard Sharp and Sgt. Major Patrick Harper from *Sharpe's Rifles* novels and the BBC series.
In the cartoon world - Dagwood Bumstead and his neighbor Herb. Homer Simpson and his neighbor Ned.
Lethal Weapons(s) – Mel Gibson and Danny Glover trust each other, though they are worlds apart in style and situation.
Lone Ranger, The and Tonto

Man of La Mancha - Don Quixote and Sancho Panza
Man Who Would Be King, The - Daniel Dravot [Sean Connery] and Peachy Carnehan [Michael Caine].
Master and Commander – Captain Jack Aubrey and Dr. Stephen Maturin.
Mickey Mouse Club TV series – the planned charm of the series was that all the Mouseketeers were great friends and invited you to be great friends with them, too.
Power of One, The
Razor's Edge, The - Larry Darrell and Gray Maturin.
Sherlock Holmes and Dr. Watson, particularly in the latest BBC Masterpiece Theatre version with Benedict Cumberbatch, and in the films with Robert Downey Jr. and Jude Law.
Sting, The – the trust between the two is there at the beginning and at the end. And probably also all through the middle, although it didn't look that way…but that was part of the sting.
Thelma and Louise - Thelma and Louise both make the decision together to go into the next realm.
Toy Story trilogy.
Tropic Thunder – Agent Matthew McConaughey's longtime friendship with Ben Stiller's Tug Speedman. Tug and Robert Downey Jr.'s Kirk Lazarus at the end form what you know will be a new BFF relationship.
In the end scene of the classic film *Casablanca*, Rick [Humphrey Bogart] says to Captain Renault [Claude Rains], "Louis, I think this is the beginning of a beautiful friendship".

And for some particular examples of the different pairings for Best Friends Forever –

Girl friends
Banger Sisters, The
Boys on the Side
First Wives Club
Fried Green Tomatoes
Heat, The – FBI agent Sandra Bullock and Boston cop Melissa McCarthy
Little Women

Mystic Pizza
Rich and Famous
Steel Magnolias
Sisterhood of the Traveling Pants
Ya-Ya Sisterhood

Boy friends/Bromance/Buddy movies
48 Hours
Batman and Robin
Boston Legal - Shatner and Spader
Clive Cussler stories – Dirk Pitt and Al Giordino
Fandango – the five college guys in this Vietnam era road movie.
Galaxy Quest
Hangover, The
Indiana Jones series – Indy and Denholm Elliott's Professor
Lawrence of Arabia and *A Dangerous Man: Lawrence after Arabia* - Lawrence and Sharif
Lethal Weapon(s)
Odd Couple, The
Point Break
Star Trek - Mister Spock, Captain Kirk, and Doctor McCoy.
Women in Love

A Guy and a Girl
Tales of the City - Mouse and Maryann
My Best Friend's Wedding
Streets of Fire - Michael Pare's Tom Cody and Amy Madigan's soldier girl McCoy
Will & Grace – TV series

Coming of Age
Stand and Deliver
Stand by Me
Young Indiana Jones – TV series - Young Indy and Remy. Indy also bonds in different episodes with Krishnamurti and T.E. Lawrence.

Examples in Music
"For Good" in *Wicked*
"I'll Be There for You" – the Rembrandts
"You've Got a Friend" – Carly Simon
"You've Got a Friend in Me" – Randy Newman, used in *Toy Story*.

Symbols
Dualities.
The clasped hands, the reaching out to each other.
Knots.

Key Element – The Shining Moment
Two (or a few more) against the rest. The action is based on mutual trust. Butch and Sundance leaping off the cliff and Thelma and Louise driving off the cliff. In *The Power of One*, the two friends are fighting the police.

Written Descriptions
You need to make the distinction between shallow friendships ala the internet and true shared-experience, shared-worldview friendships from real life. The 2012 expose of Notre Dame football player Teo and his imaginary internet girlfriend is an example of the former. The *Thelma and Louise* relationship is an example of the latter. The distinction is an emotional commitment that can be realized in real physical action and presence. Can your character say to their friend, "I'll be there for you" and really do it?

Life is a series of cycles and real friends go through them together, helping each other start over, renew their enthusiasm, make it through the hard times, etc. When something horrible or fabulous happens, "Who you gonna call?" It's going to be your real friends. When friends actually show up on the doorstep in person, that's BFF. When they go with you on some crazy mission, like in *My Best Friend's Wedding,* that's BFF.

In shallow relationships there is no beginning, no end, just the fleeting participation of the moment, a chuckle at a clever quip, or an LOL at a funny cat video.

Finishing each other's sentences.

Knowing what the other is thinking and wants to do.

They'll often dress like each other and then when they show up in matching outfits say, "What are we, in fifth grade?"

They like the same things, or if not, they tease each other good-naturedly about it.

They'll stand up for each other and stand between danger and each other.

Link them by name when possible: "Jason and Steve ran to the edge" rather than "Jason ran to the edge. Steve followed."

Cinematic Techniques
The clasped hands, the reaching out to each other.

Arm in arm.

The hug in Bromance stories. The friendly punch in the arm. Giving noogies.

The physical embrace. See the wrestling-nude-in-the-firelight scene between Rupert and Gerald in *Women in Love.*

Shoot them side-by-side, on equal angles so as not to over-emphasize one or the other.

Circle the camera around the two of them to make a visual cocoon as they look out at whatever enchants or endangers them.

Conclusion

The qualities of the BFF relationship are love, loyalty, and camaraderie based on total acceptance. It is non-judgmental about each other's bad behaviours. It is always supportive. It is long-lasting even when separated by time and place.

The BFF is a comfort and an inspiration. In your stories these friends can offer support and can straighten out your heroine when she is getting off track.

*****

Exercise #1 – Awareness
Who are your favourite examples of BFF in history, myth, or current real life?

*****

Exercise #2 – Writing
Write a version of the scene you have chosen with the characters as strangers. Then write it with the same people as long-time Best Friends Forever.

*****

Further Reading
Inner Drives – Pamela Jaye Smith
Little Women
Power of the Dark Side - Pamela Jaye Smith
Symbols.Images.Codes - Pamela Jaye Smith
Sisterhood of the Traveling Pants
Women in Love   *Ya-Ya Sisterhood, The*

Further Viewing
Big Chill, The   *Blue Crush*
Four Feathers, The   *Friends* – TV series
Importance of Being Earnest, The
New Girl, The – TV series
Sex and the City – TV series
Talented Mr. Ripley, The
Tales of the City – TV series
Two Broke Girls – TV series

CHAPTER FOUR

WARRIOR BONDING

We few, we happy few, we band of brothers;
For he to-day that sheds his blood with me
Shall be my brother; be he ne'er so vile,
This day shall gentle his condition;
And gentlemen in England now-a-bed
Shall think themselves accurs'd they were not here,
And hold their manhoods cheap whiles any speaks
That fought with us upon Saint Crispin's day.

Henry V
William Shakespeare

Warrior bonding is a very special kind of Love. It only occurs between people who have faced great danger together, who have shared the fear, the sense of adventure, the fierce protectiveness of each other, the bewildering relief when the danger has passed, and the spectrum of returning home to a hero's welcome or to not being appreciated by the very people they fought to save.

Though typically warrior bonding is forged when you're being shot at, it is often enough to know that you might be attacked, bombed, etc. In the long-running hit TV series M*A*S*H*, most of the action was at the field hospital. The danger was over the Korean hills from which there was always the possibility of stray artillery or a direct attack on their camp.

This kind of love is most often a heightened version of the BFF Best Friends Forever and a variation on Family Love with a lot of Love of Country thrown in. It's a heady mix and is bound to deeply affect your characters.

Combat veterans will sometimes admit that they love their war buddies more than their spouses and their children. There is something so very intense about that bond that makes it stand out from all others.

The Defining Myth
The Knights of the Round Table were bound by oaths of loyalty, belief in the rightness of their actions centering around the nobility of King Arthur and his vision for peace, and later their Quest for the elusive Holy Grail. Knights forged strong bonds with each other in Camelot and out slaying dragons and saving damsels and would come to each other's aid in an instant.

Exemplar Movies
Star Trek Into Darkness, Camelot, Tropic Thunder, The Wild Bunch, Magnificent Seven, Seven Samurai, Dawn Patrol

Why it exists (evolutionary back-story)
Survival is easier when you're not alone. Also, there is a synergistic effect where the whole is greater than the sum of the parts. Whether you're hunting dangerous animals or fighting off an invading army, teamwork carries the day.

The Warrior Caste is a unique and separate group within a culture, just as are the priesthood, the government, the educators, the healers, the artists, etc. This distinct division of labour typically forms at earlier stages of cultural development than the others.

How it works (physiology & psychology)
The heightened adrenalin of fight-or-flight situations creates deep impressions on the mind. The amygdala which processes fear affects many other parts of the brain; this effect can be seen in PTSD (post traumatic stress disorder).

Military training strips down individuality then creates teams. All you have in battle are those few soldiers right beside you. Some fellow warriors are people you might not like at all in regular life, but you are bonded by the necessity of collaboration for survival.

Shared intense experiences create strong common bonds that can last a lifetime.

How it serves us now
The tools of war have gotten more sophisticated and allow people to fight from safer distances. There's not very much warrior bonding going on between drone pilots sitting in cool cubicles on a military base in Arizona. In the hills of Afghanistan, yes.

Heroic events also happen without being shot at. Actions for the greater good must be involved while facing a large danger such as natural disasters or hostile groups of people. Police seldom deploy in more than groups of two, sometimes these days just one, but SWAT teams and bomb squads have more potential for warrior bonding. Firefighters typically protect just a portion of a city and are usually working to save property and rescue people. This shouldn't make firefighters seem less than. Certainly the firefighters who ran into the WTC, up scores of flights of stairs, and died to save others did it willingly and on the fly. Those who survived are no doubt bonded forever with each other. The TV series *Rescue Me* centers on the loving bond between those firefighters.

On a smaller scale non-warriors can experience some aspects of this Warrior Love when they share stressful situations that demand teamwork, a common cause, and personal sacrifice such as in team sports.

The Warrior Archetype has been weakened of late by fighting unwinnable wars, imperialist actions for extraction capitalism, and co-opting the term "warrior" for such ignoble causes as holiday shopping and business travel. Regardless, the Warrior Bonding can still occur.

Do keep in mind that old saying of Honour Among Thieves – even your bad guys can share Warrior Love.

Examples in Myth and Legend

The Arthurian cycle of myths centering on the KNIGHTS OF THE ROUND TABLE. Tennyson's *Idylls of the King* is one of the best sources for these stories.

JASON AND THE ARGONAUTS – some of the guys on this quest for the Golden Fleece were already closely knit by familial or romantic ties, but the dangers of the journey forged strong bonds among them all, except for a few who strayed off and one who was left behind because he was sick and smelled bad. Tomboy Atalanta was also on the quest and bested the guys in most warrior skills.

In the *Iliad* it's more individuals out for themselves and the Greeks are particularly fractious, but the relationship between the hero Achilles and his beloved cousin Patroclus was especially close and was the trigger for a major turning point in the story. Achilles was pouting in his tent and his absence from the battlefield allowed the Trojans to gain ground. Patroclus put on Achilles armor, rallied the troops, and went up against the Trojan hero Hector. But Hector killed him and took the armor for himself. Wracked by grief, Achilles took the field again to avenge his beloved warrior-cousin-friend: This roused the Greeks, who ultimately won the war. Achilles slayed Hector, then died himself, to be re-united in Hades with Patroclus.

The Amazon warrior women were bound to each other by philosophy and their unusual cultural set-up – they only used men to make babies and were said to have let the male babies die. Men were the enemy and no quarter was given. Except in a few instances they all lived to regret, including Hercules and Theseus who infiltrated and seduced away some of the women and Belerophon who conquered them.

The Norse Valkyries were war goddesses bonded in their mission to pluck dying warriors from the battlefields and carry them lovingly up to Valhalla, the warrior heaven where they ate, drank, and partied for eternity.

Examples in History and Current Events
Alexander the Great inspired such strong loyalties among his soldiers that they followed him all the way from Macedonia to India and back.

Julius Caesar and Marc Antony were battle buddies and then empire builders together until separated by love for the same woman, Cleopatra Queen of Egypt.

We typically think of warrior bonding between males. But what about women and women? Or women and men?

Boedicea was queen of the Britons who led her people to victory against the invading Roman Empire.

As our current day military begins to become more inclusive there will be more warrior bonding between men and women.

Doctors and nurses in war zones, like the warriors, form strong bonds from shared danger and serving a higher cause. The TV series *M*A*S*H* and *China Beach* poignantly tell many of those stories.

Examples in Media

Spock and Kirk in *Star Trek Into Darkness*. Both of them defy regulations to save each other. The telling scene is when they place their hands against either side of the window of the radiation decompression chamber and hold a pure, loving look. Both now know they would always be there for each other, no matter what.

Battlestar Galactica has some of the best Warrior Love ever on many levels between many characters. *Babylon 5* is also rich with that special type of love.

Titus Pullo and Lucius Vorenus in HBO's *Rome*.

Sharpe's Rifles and *Game of Thrones* both feature Sean Bean and are both rich with Warrior Bonding.

Check out Walter Hill's *Southern Comfort* for a really hot look between endangered National Guard warriors Powers Booth and Keith Carradine.

In *Zulu*, a small group of British soldiers fights Zulu tribesmen in South Africa and a number of them survive, even winning the respect of their enemy for being such worthy opponents.

In the first three *Star Wars* movies Luke Skywalker, Princess Leia, Han Solo, Chewbacca, R2D2 and C3P0 are Warrior-bonded in their fight against Darth Vader, the Emperor, and the evil Empire.

The characters in *Courage Under Fire* exhibit warrior bonding, but after Captain Walden's (Meg Ryan) death, the group mentality dissolves into every man covering his own ass.

Artists and entertainers who served in the military often carried a special popularity which we might well call Warrior Bonding between those on the stage and screen and their fellow military comrades out in the audience. When selecting a film to see, veterans may be more inclined to choose one starring a fellow veteran.

Musicians include: John Philip Sousa, Rudy Vallee, Glenn Miller, Dave Brubeck, Elvis Presley, Kris Kristofferson, Josephine Baker (served in the French Resistance), and many more.

Actors include Abbott and Costello, Eddie Albert, Alan Alda of the popular long-running *M*A*S*H**, James Arness of *Gunsmoke*, Charles Durning, Gene Autry, Jimmy Stewart, Donald Duck and Bugs Bunny (Bugs was given an official service record in the U.S. Marine Corps), Bill Cosby, Buddy Ebsen (Coast Guard), Douglas Fairbanks Jr., Henry Fonda, Clark Gable, James Garner, Arthur Godfrey, Bob Hope, Lee Marvin, Ed McMahon, Audie Murphy (most decorated soldier of WWII), Tyrone Power, Jason Robards, George C. Scott (who later became Patton in the movie of the same name), James Whitmore, Montel Williams, Jonathan Winters, and many more.

Examples in Music
"American Soldier" – Toby Keith
"Angel Flight" - Radney Foster
"Ballad of the Green Berets" from the movie *Green Berets*
"Over the Hills and Far Away" – *Sharpe's Rifles* TV series
"Panzerlied" – the Panzer Song, *Battle of the Bulge* [check out the further stanzas at end of this YouTube video]
Songs of the Spanish Civil War

Symbols
Swords
Flags
Crossed rifles
Clasped hands
Carrying a wounded comrade
Slogans
Huddled together under fire

Key Element – The Shining Moment
Facing the battle, the fire, the villain and proceeding forward anyway. Not alone, but with the "band of brothers".

Pulling the comrade out of harm's way, carrying her to safety.

Jumping in to take the hit and save others, as Woody Harrelson did in *Thin Red Line*.

Comforting wounded and dying comrades.

A blood-brother oath where the individuals ritually cut themselves and mix their blood.

Written Descriptions
Use words such as: band, banded, band of brothers or sisters, groups, troop, company, come together, etc. to denote the unity of the individuals.

Rather than listing the individual names all the time, in moments of emotion and action that embody the concept of Warrior Bonding, call them by the name of their group: Easy Company, Chosen Men, the Brotherhoods, 2/5, the club, the ladies, etc.

Tell us about the strength of the bonds. Is it "We always bring back our dead, we never leave a brother behind" or "Every man for himself"?

Use the group's slogan because of the shared identity associated with it: "Remember the Alamo", "Retreat, Hell", "Gary Owen" (Irish regiments always shouted it as they were going over the wall). Look up the slogans of the Scottish clans, and of military regiments around the world. Slogans both reflect and add to the creation and refinement of the myth of group. The movie *We Were Soldiers* uses a lot of these to advance character development and to further illustrate the bonding between soldiers.

Have an outsider comment about the warriors. "When these men were young, they saved the world", said President Bill Clinton in Normandy at a D-Day event honouring the men who stormed the beaches and helped end WWII, as portrayed in *Saving Private Ryan*.

Cinematic Techniques
Shooting from the deck in an up-angle to the group charging into the fray; this angle will increase the audience perception of your characters as being larger-than-life. This can denote them being on a higher (usually the Aspirational Solar Plexus) chakra with the commitment to each other and their cause, not just to sheer survival at the lower Root chakra. The head takes up most of the frame, the steep up-angle indicates their commitment -- "I'm going to go kill the enemy, save my fellow soldiers, and protect my country".

Or as in *Henry V, Independence Day*, and *Patton*, place the person giving the inspiring speech up higher than the others. And show the reverse angle of the troops looking up at the speaker. This posture and angle promotes the worshipful attitude in many of the soldiers towards their leaders.

Show arms going over shoulders in a comradely way. A two-shot of soldiers cradling their wounded brothers as in *Thin Red Line* when Witt is a medic tending to bloodied soldiers in the river.

Wide angle of entire battlefield, then push in to small clusters of the group.

Conclusion
This kind of love can be the magnet that brings disparate people together and the glue that keeps them together in the face of overwhelming opposition.

Warrior Love can be the culmination of personal trials and character arcs taking someone to a higher level of commitment and sacrifice.

When you write about Warrior Bonding you are touching upon one of the strongest emotions humans experience. It is forged in the fires of danger and death. It is about loyalty, it is about sacrificing one's self for the other and for the greater good.

*****

Exercise #1 – Awareness
What is the strongest instance of Warrior Love you can name from myth, history, media, or real life?

*****

Exercise #2 – Writing
Write an exchange of 5-6 lines of dialogue between a troubled warrior who cannot open up to a civilian loved one.

Re-write the scene with the troubled warrior opening up to a beloved fellow warrior.

*****

Further Reading
Art of War, The by Sun Tzu - Samuel B. Griffith
Awakened Warrior, The - Rick Fields, Editor
Book of Five Rings, The - Miyamoto Musashi / Victor Harris
Campaigns of Alexander, The - Arrian
Civil War, The - Julius Caesar
Descartes' Error - Antonio R. Damasio
Dictionary of Military Terms - Arcos
Don Juan, The series - Carlos Castenada
Heroines - Norma Lorre Goodrich
Infantry Attacks - General Erwin Rommel
Killer Angels, The - Michael Shaara
Leadership and the New Science - Margaret J. Wheatley
Lincoln on Leadership - Donald T. Phillips
Mysteries of Mithras, The - Franz Cumont
Origin of Consciousness in the Breakdown of the Bi-cameral Mind, The - Julian Jaynes
General George S. Patton, Jr. - books by and about
Red Team, Green Team, etc. – Richard "Demo Dicky" Marcinko
Roots of Strategy - Brig. General T.R. Phillips

Shamballa, Sacred Path of the Warrior - Chogyam Trungpa
Super Faculties and their Culture - Manly P. Hall
Warriors' Words, Quotations - Peter G. Tsourus
Women Warriors, A History - David E. Jones

Further Viewing
Apocalypse Now
Band of Brothers
Battle of Los Angeles
Born on the 4th of July
Braveheart
Brothers – Danish film
Coming Home
Deerhunter
Dune - especially the Fremen
Full Metal Jacket
G.I. Jane
Galaxy Quest
Henry V
Hercules – TV series starring Kevin Sorbo
Hurt Locker, The
Platoon
Private Benjamin
Purple Heart
Red Dawn
Saving Private Ryan
Star Trek(s)
Starship Troopers
Stripes
The Best Years of Our Lives
Tropic Thunder
We Were Soldiers
Xena: Warrior Princess
Zero Dark Thirty
Zulu

Web links
Alpha Babe Academy
http://alphababeacademy.com

First Earth Battalion
http://www.firstearthbattalion.com

Joseph Campbell Foundation
www.jcf.org

MYTHWORKS
www.mythworks.net

Air War College
http://www.au.af.mil/au/awc/

Army War College
http://www.carlisle.army.mil/usawc/about/aboutUs.cfm

National War College
http://www.ndu.edu/nwc/index.cfm

National Defense University
http://www.ndu.edu/

Navy War College
http://www.usnwc.edu/

Royal Military Academy, England
http://www.army.mod.uk/training_education/training/17057.asp
x

West Point Military Academy
http://www.usma.edu/SitePages/Home.aspx

CHAPTER FIVE

LOVE FOR ANIMALS

Out of the earth
I sing for them
a Horse nation...
I sing for them
Out of the earth
I sing for them
the animals...
I sing for them.

Teton Sioux Indians

Awwww, isn't it precious!

Some of the purest love on the planet is for and from our pets. Except for cats, who obviously consider humans fortunate if the cat pays it any attention at all.

Some of the most unconditional love some humans can bestow is upon their pets. Which is sad as those people often only seem able to relate to animals, not to other humans.

Pets are often thought of as members of the family. Depending on the family in your story, the pets may be more affectionate and loyal than some of the humans.

You know the saying that people and their dogs look alike? What kind of dog would your Protagonist have? Your Antagonist?

As opposed to pure animals, humans-as-animals such as werewolves and mermaids is a different kind of love and will be touched upon in a later Lesson.

The Defining Myth
In *The Odyssey*, when Odysseus returns home from Troy to Ithaca after a twenty year absence it is only his faithful old dog Argo who recognizes his much older, travel-worn master. Argo wags his tail, limps over and licks Odysseus's calloused hand, then dies, content that they had at last been reunited.

Exemplar Movie
The Jungle Book

Why it exists (evolutionary back-story)
The domestication of animals is one of the biggest leaps in cultural development in the history of humanoids, going way back to Cro-Magnon and Neanderthals at least.

Most humans must interact somehow with the local fauna. Depending on the ferocity, timidity, and taste of those animals, they were feared, became friends or food.

While a number of mythologies give humans dominion over animals, it is relatively few animal species that have ever been tamed. We still share the planet with thousands of species that could care less about humans and who basically ignore us, until our actions affect their well-being.

Animals in the wild do exhibit unique characteristics which have become examples in folklore on how to understand humanity. The hive-mind of bees is like the mob-mind of rampaging humans. Human predation from the sexual to the financial reflects the prey-predator symbiosis of lions and wildebeest.

The pack hierarchy of wolves and other canines is reflected in the structure of many societies, militaries, and businesses.

How it works (physiology & psychology)
Most animals are downright adorable in their youth. Just like with human babies, it's part of Nature's way to ensure we don't just toss out the mewling, crying, messy little things in a fit of fatigue or pique. The sense of protecting and nurturing a vulnerable creature plugs into our need to be needed.

Puppies build empathy in kids. It is important for a child to have a pet to take care of when they are very young, as the brain wiring for empathy needs to be set in the first 5-7 years. If not developed early on, it's just not there. If the empathy does not get wired in they will never be able to have healthy relationships with other humans or animals, which is part of the problem with child soldiers and kids in slums and refugee camps. The sensitivities of other humans and creatures are alien to them.

Kids who torture animals may well become serial killers.

Unfortunately for some people they do not have loving and sustaining relationships with other humans. For some, the relationship with a pet is the only available substitute. You can create an effective character arc by taking a person from pets-only relating to being able to relate in a more healthy way to other humans. When they stumble or face a set-back, how they interact with the animal can reflect that.

Pre-teen girls have a propensity for horses, the psychology of which is exceedingly analyzed and ranges from the safe-yet-powerful creature that is tame to their own beck-and-call to the physical stimulation of riding, though typically the naive girls do not know why it feels so good.

The value of human to animal relationships cannot be dismissed. Whether they represent a metaphor for the character, offer an opportunity for the character to relate to something outside themselves, or give them a chance to access their childhood, this animal-to-human connection can be a strong and powerful force of revelation and motivation for your character.

How it serves us now
Hunting animals have worked alongside humans for millennia, be they falcons, pointers, fox-hounds, carrier pigeons, etc. Though they are not necessarily thought of as pets, domesticated animals have moved human progress forward by leaps and bounds. Where would we be without cattle, chickens, pigs and sheep, draft animals such as horses and oxen. Many of those do become pets for kids living on farms and ranches, though that country lifestyle is rare these days.

Professional dogs are trained to sniff out various things: escaped prisoners, illegal substances, bombs, cancer, impending epileptic fits, etc. Their skills and focused dedication save thousands of lives each year.

More and more these days rescue dogs are sent in to search for humans trapped in collapsed buildings! One even went on the Bin Ladin raid.

Service dogs bring mobility and close companionship to the blind, and they've been known to help solve some mysteries in books and media, too.

Medical science has proven that having a cat or dog to pet is helpful to recuperation from illness and to control blood pressure. Many rehab units and retirement homes have in-house pets who wander around the place interacting with the patients to the betterment of all.

The keeping of colourful songbirds in charmingly constructed cages is a hobby for many older gentlemen in parts of Asia. They gather with their birds in open-air restaurants in a rainbow palette of sight and song.

And then there are the farm animal contests at county fairs and the international contests for best-in-show where human pride rather than love may well be the main driver.

Examples in Myth and Legend
The first card in the Tarot deck Major Arcana is "The Fool". A naive young man, travel bag and staff over his shoulder, is about to step off a cliff and into the great unknown for what he obviously thinks will be a merry adventure. There's a small white dog traveling with him. The dog's name is "Argo" and variously represents exuberance and love for life, loyalty, innocence, and the need to start any great undertaking at an elemental level.

Many mythologies combine human and animal traits to come up with exotic creatures such as the sphinx, centaurs, chimeras, and the animal gods of dynastic Egypt.

Witches and wizards usually have an animal "familiar". Harry Potter's is the owl. A black cat is the traditional knowledgeable creature who is a messenger for the magic-maker.

Rudyard Kipling's *Jungle Book* is a charming adventure in interspecies bonding between Mowgli the human boy and the many jungle creatures, as well as between the creatures themselves.

Examples in History and Current Events
English King Charles II during the Restoration period always had the little "foot-warmer" Corgis around him and they have remained the dog of choice for the English royal family.

Genghis Khan and his Mongol Horde conquered a huge part of Asia, the Far East, the Middle East, and the Near East on the swift and sturdy Mongolian ponies, treasuring them often more than their wives.

PETA – People for the Ethical Treatment of Animals – has pressured change in many industries, including media production ala the "no animal was harmed" disclaimer. Their beliefs and actions, sometimes radical, are rich fodder for dramatic conflict. Save the Whales, Greenpeace, and other animal rights organizations dedicate resources to protecting various animals. They too offer opportunities for conflict in your stories.

While working to protect animals from the ill-will or ignorance of humans is admirable, pet-love can also get way out of hand in the other direction. E.g. the "handbag barkers" of celebrity show-offs, the heiress who leaves her millions to her cats (an action just begging for probating the will), or the unlicensed amateur breeder who keeps 26 Dalmatian pups in her house and is busted by the SPCA.

Working dogs can lead the blind, sniff out epileptic attacks and cancer, keep elderly people company and lower their blood pressure, and help humans in many other ways.

K-9 law enforcement dogs form very strong bonds with their human partners.

And then there's that old saying, often proven true, that people resemble their pets, and vice versa.

Examples in Media
There is a long history of pets in cinema, perhaps because they play such a big part in so many people's lives, and in great part no doubt because they evoke such strong emotions.

In animation some animals are pets, some are anthropomorphized animals. Some communicate with humans but remain animals, such as Lassie, who was always able to get across to others that, "Timmy has fallen into the well!"

In the very popular 1982 E.T. movie the young boy was protective of the little alien and treated him like somebody's loveable lost pet.

Other animals that bond with humans are King Kong, Mighty Joe Young, and Godzilla. In the Matthew Broderick version Godzilla the huge ape sniffs Broderick and then recognizes him throughout the story.

Watch the documentary on the making of *Winged Migration* to see humans who love, care for, and communicate with birds. This "making-of" feature is way more interesting than the film itself.

A famous human-animal friendship is that of Tarzan and his pal Cheetah the chimp. Roy Rogers had Bullet [a dog] and Trigger [a horse] who usually played into the story line of the movies and TV series. His wife and adventure partner Dale Evans had a horse named Buttermilk

Stories sometimes have animals talking to animals in the presence of humans, like in *Beverly Hills Chihuahua*. Generally the humans don't know they can talk so you can put a lot of insight, wisdom, and humour into the mouths of the critters.

Mythical, mystical, and totally imagined animals populate many fantasy, sci-fi, and supernatural stories. You can take great liberties with how the creatures look and what they do, as was so well done in *Avatar* with the horses and the dragons, and the ferocious creatures, too. In *Game of Thrones* it's dragons.

YouTube is crowded with animal videos, from interspecies bonding to talking dogs to cute kittens.

And really, you've got to have Scooby-Doo in here.

Examples in Music
"If I could talk to the animals" from Dr. Doolittle
"I Wanna Be Like You" from Jungle Book
Mister Ed theme song – 1960s TV series
"Wildfire" – Michael Martin Murphy

Symbols
The animal itself is often the symbol for a character's personality: brave like a lion, crafty like a fox, soft as a kitten, loyal as a dog, etc.

Leashes and cages represent control and confinement.

Bared teeth and bloody claws can indicate ferocity.

The animal pelt often points to humans conquering some aspects of Mother Nature, as with Hercules who wears a lion skin. Typically the animals are predators, and are worn by warriors. You don't see many hippo head masks.

Key Element – The Shining Action
Recognition - The moment when the faithful pet recognizes the master no one else knows, like with Argo and Odysseus reunited after twenty years. To build up the tension take three steps towards this.

1) The pet's ears perk up, "Is that a familiar voice?" The dog in *Memphis Belle* knows the sound of the B-17 bomber's engines.

2) They sniff the air trying to analyze the elusive scent. In the *Chronicles of Riddick* the guard beasts on Crematoria recognize "something" about Riddick, who says, "It's an animal thing".

3) After a moment or two of indecision, full recognition sweeps over both the animal and the human and they reunite in a release of heartfelt emotion, as in *Warhorse* when the horse recognizes the kid's whistling and goes to him.

This can also work for the Antagonist by having the animal reject or attack the bad guy. *Enemy of the State* has a little yapper dog who's bitten the CIA agent trying to bug Will Smith. The wound troubles him throughout the rest of the movie.

In *Payback*, a huge guard dog named after the character Porter is a trap for the bad guy looking for Porter. He's pointed into the next room and attacked by the dog. The dog gets shot trying to save his master.

Revelation - The animal leads the humans to learn something they would not otherwise have known about. Perhaps the dog smells the dead body. Or as in an episode of the Canadian TV series *Murdoch Mysteries,* a parrot helps identify a murderer. Animals can dig up treasure, pluck it off mountains, gallop down seemingly wrong roads only to discover fantastic places, etc.

Protection - Animals protecting humans calls forth a strong, primitive response in us of appreciation, recognition of our innate oneness as life-forms on the planet, and the inherent nobility of some creatures. Some examples are dolphins saving drowning swimmers; Hooch dies protecting Turner in *Turner and Hooch*, but also leaves a litter of pups behind; the dire wolves of *Game of Thrones* protecting the Stark children; dogs staying by their felled owners [unlike cats who'd just as soon eat them....not that cats don't have lots of other redeeming qualities].

Written Descriptions

How do the characters talk *about* the animals and how do they talk *to* the animals? Show us emotions and motives behind both. Is it a harsh voice or a gentle voice; respectful or dismissive? Think of the difference between someone who runs a game preserve versus a hunter just out for a bragging-rights trophy, as in the British TV series *Wild at Heart.*

Do the animals talk to each other like in *Babe, Charlotte's Web*, and *Winnie the Pooh*? If you anthropomorphize animals, give them each a unique voice and point of view, just as you would your human characters.

Do the animals actually speak to the people in your story, like in *The Chronicles of Narnia* and in many myths? Or is the communication telepathic like in *Dragonriders of Pern* and in the minds of many pet owners. How clear are those lines of communication? What happens when something is lost in translation?

When using action verbs be sure to give us an adverb to let us know the emotion behind that action. E.g., He whips the horse gently. He whips the horse cruelly. He reinforces the training with a flick of the whip.

With all due respect to Blake Snyder's *Save the Cat* series of books for screenwriters, there's a lot more drama about a person who does *not* save the cat. A story in which the animal does not win or survive can be very dramatic as in the classic mid-century film *Old Yeller,* where the beloved and heroic dog has to be put down. Then there was the pet bunny who got boiled in *Fatal Attraction*. The animal's demise became the code phrase for stalking. The threat of an animal being killed can heighten the drama and serve the larger story arc.

When appropriate, tell us about the animal's emotions. E.g. The cat hisses angrily. The kitten purrs affectionately.

Cinematic Techniques
Shoot from the animal's POV [Point of View]. Is it the pig *Babe* or the elephant *Babar*? That point of view determines how the animal character perceives the world and their place in it. You give us a sense of who they are by showing us their perspective. You can use it when they are "talking" so we see the reactions to their words. You can also use this angle to bring attention to something important in the plot or dialogue. It can be about a lesson being taught.

When shooting an animal's POV – depending on your style and genre – consider showing us how they actually see things. Dogs see mostly in black and white, birds and insects see infrared, flies see with a thousand facets. For more on how different animals see --
http://webecoist.momtastic.com/2009/01/14/animal-vision-color-detection-and-color-blindness/

Shoot from alongside the animal, which lends itself to the conversational mode. It also demonstrates the relationship between the animal and other characters. E.g. in the old TV series *Mr. Ed*, the horse Ed and his human Wilbur are shot with their heads at the same level, implying equality between the two.

Use a CU [Close Up] on some part of the animal's anatomy that is symbolic of their character or situation: a snake shedding its skin, a glossy or mangy coat, healthy or wounded legs or feet, etc.

Use the ECU [Extreme Close Up] on the animal's eyes (one, two, or a thousand eyes) just as you would use an ECU on human eyes - to reveal intensity and fire, a shift in attitude presaging a shift in action, some heretofore hidden aspect of their nature, etc.

Conclusion

Keep in mind that secondary and tertiary characters are there to reveal something about your main characters. Use a pet or other animal to reveal some personality trait, a quirk, or an otherwise hidden agenda. Think of the dog in the charming animated film UP; he tells us so much about the characters by the way he interacts with them, from his grumpy old owner Carl to the young scout Russell to the evil Charles Muntz.

Use animals to symbolize psychological aspects of your characters.

Use them as conduits to get characters to interact. It's a "well known fact" that a guy walking a cute dog is a "chick magnet".

If it does fit in with your story's style, keep in mind the inherent dignity of animals, their special intelligences, and their often rich personalities. They can be special story characters in their own right.

*****

Exercise #1 – Awareness

What is the most unusual pet or humanoid/animal relationship you can name from myth, history, media, or real life?

*****

Exercise #2 – Writing

Select/write a short scene that has one type of animal active in the story line. Change the animal and write the same scene but with the influence of the quite different creature: a parrot and then a python, a cat then a hamster, a dragon and then a goldfish, etc.

*****

Further Reading

Aesop's Fables
Animals in Translation - Temple Grandin
Dragonriders of Pern – the entire series by Anne McCaffrey
Horse Whisperer, The – Nicholas Evans
Inner Drives – Pamela Jaye Smith

Power of the Dark Side – Pamela Jaye Smith
Symbol and Symbolic – Schwaller de Lubicz [Egyptian animal symbology]
Symbols.Images.Codes – Pamela Jaye Smith

Further Viewing
Aristocats, the
Benji
Best in Show
Beverly Hills Chihuahua
Beethoven
Black Beauty
Budweiser Clydesdale Super Bowl commercial
Dr. Doolittle
Finding Nemo
Flipper – TV series
Fly Away Home
Horse Whisperer, The
How to Train Your Dragon
K-911
Lady and the Tramp, The
Lassie
Little Mermaid, The
Marley & Me
Mister Ed
My Friend Flicka
National Velvet
Old Yeller
Payback
Rin Tin Tin
Secretariat
Show Chickens http://www.videolala.com/watch-showchickens-2001
Turner and Hooch
War Horse
Wild at Heart

CHAPTER SIX

LOVE OF ART

Morning fields of amber grain
Weathered faces lined in pain
Are soothed beneath the artist's
loving hand

"Vincent" (Starry Starry Night)
Don McLean

Your characters, even in romantic comedies, supernatural romances, or historical novels, will be richer for having other interests than just romantic or sexual love. Show us real people with real lives and professions, vocations and callings, passions and drives. If those are focused on the Arts you can then bring more unexpected, idealistic, and emotional elements into your storyline.

Since art touches all of us in some way or another – either viewing or experiencing it in sculpture, painting, music, writing, dance, media, games – you will gain another connection from your story to your audience.

The Defining Myths
Pygmalion was a young Greek sculptor who was disappointed in love. He decided to have nothing more to do with girls. So instead he carved the perfect girl in marble, named her Galatea, and fell in love with her. In some of the stories he even dressed her up and had "tea parties" with her. At a feast of Aphrodite he made a fervent wish that his great work of art would come alive so he could enjoy his perfect love, Galatea. Impressed by his devotion, Aphrodite granted him his desire and the marble statue warmed, quickened, and stepped down off the pedestal and into his arms. According to most of the stories, happiness ensued between the artist and his art.

Competition between artists can also be quite dramatic. Although the Greco-Roman goddess Pallas Athena invented the flute, she didn't like the way she looked when she played it – cheeks all puffed out and lips pursed. So she threw it away. A satyr, Marsyas, found it and had quite a talent for music. He received a lot of praise and got rather pompous. He even had the gall to challenge Athena's half-brother Apollo, the god of music, healing, light, and truth. Rather stupid of a lowly satyr to go up against a god...as he soon found out. Of course Apollo won the music contest. To punish the upstart Marsyas, Apollo had him flayed – skinned alive by whipping.

Exemplar Movies
Amadeus, Shakespeare in Love, Moulin Rouge, The Agony and the Ecstasy

Why it exists (evolutionary back-story)
Archeology and paleo-anthropology have pushed back the origins of art to around 70,000 years ago. The conscious creation of things of beauty and meaning seems to be what separates us most from the animals, though that may be in question as we learn more about them and how their brains work.

See more in Werner Herzog's film *Cave of Forgotten Dreams*.

How it works (physiology & psychology)

The desire to create seems built into our human psyche. Throughout much of human history women were naturally creative in that they made new human beings, a miraculous-seeming accomplishment still today. Males, driven by a similar inherent need to create but lacking the natural process of baby-making, tended to be the artists, the inventors, the explorers, the conquerors. Most of those drives are in their most basic form, the imperative to create something new and to leave one's personal mark on the world. Societies have not historically been kind to women who have taken up the arts, but that seems to be greatly improving across the world.

Art can alter our state of being and take us outside the daily concerns of physical existence. It can bring us peace, inspiration, contemplation, exaltation. It is no wonder so many religions incorporate art into their rituals, be it music, icons, uplifting architecture, poetry, dance, etc.

Ethnic music and dance help unite a people around their tribal core. It helps create an actual physical unification of the individuals to the group through rhythms and tones and the effect those have on the actual physical body.

THE MUSE - That which sets artists apart from others has been attributed to genius, to being touched by the gods, to being slightly crazy, often including severe mood swings. Many artists have a Muse who inspires them.

Sometimes the Muse is an immortal. The nine Greek Muses were daughters of king god Zeus and Mnemosyne, or Memory. They included Polyhymnia the Muse of songs to the gods, Calliope of epic poetry, Euterpe of lyric poetry, Melpomene of tragedy, Thalia of comedy, Terpsichore of dance, and Erato of love poetry.

Sometimes the Muse is an unobtainable love object, such as the married Ladies [often a queen] in Provencal poetry and in the Arthurian tales of the Knights of the Round Table. Sometimes the Muse is an actual mortal lover, as is the case with many artists and sculptors.

The Muse inspires, connects the artist to higher ideals, and helps them step away from the regular world into the heady world of art and its creation. The Muse opens you up to raise yourself to a higher level. They are the trigger and the conduit for inspiration and artistic focus but you still have to do the work. It's not like an angel giving you a miracle, you still have to pick up the palette, the hammer and chisel, put your fingers on the keyboard, etc.

When one has lost touch with the Muse, the art stops. Then the search for the lost Muse or for a new Muse begins. The premise of *Shakespeare in Love* is this search for the Muse.

Do not try to domesticate the Muse. When relegated to housekeeping, child bearing, and quotidian chores they no longer hold that higher, ethereal, artistic frequency so necessary for creation. As Robert Graves notes in *The White Goddess*, love your Muse but never marry her, or him. See more about this in *Inner Drives*, the chapter on "Marilyns, Moms, and Muses".

You can however have sex with the Muse. Often rather amazing sex. The sex act and the creative act are similar, but one is not necessarily a guarantee of the other. Sex can be uplifting physically and emotionally, but a Muse should raise your thought processes up to a higher level. The artist with a sex partner completes the physical act. But with a Muse there is no "completion" until you have finished creating the art.

Mythologist Joseph Campbell talks a lot about the muse and his work is well worth looking into.

There's a new Estee Lauder fragrance called Modern Muse. The logline is – "Be an Inspiration".

There are three ways to relate to art: create it, critique it, appreciate it. In the chakra system the artistic creator operates from the Throat chakra, home of conscious creativity. The critic may also operate from there via their logical analysis and deconstruction of a piece of art. The critic will often also be coming from the Lower Solar Plexus with a heavy dose of envy. The audience that appreciates art can do so from different chakras. In the Aspirational Solar Plexus position they can be uplifted and transformed; in the Sacral chakra they can be titillated, depressed or frightened; and they can be driven to action from the Root or Lower Solar Plexus position.

How it serves us now

Art can enlighten. It carries meaning across time and culture: e.g. the stained glass windows of Gothic cathedrals visually presented the Bible stories to an illiterate congregation.

Art divides people as much as it unites them. The battle still rages over how to define beauty and art. What's important to you is that it is still considered an important issue and can provide good story background.

Art can inspire. There's a great scene in *The Shawshank Redemption* where Mozart's music plays over the prison loudspeakers, bringing exquisite moments of joy, flight, freedom, and beauty to the prisoners. Morgan Freeman's Red says, "I have no idea to this day what those two Italian ladies were singing about. Truth is, I don't want to know. Some things are best left unsaid. I'd like to think they were singing about something so beautiful, it can't be expressed in words, and makes your heart ache because of it. I tell you, those voices soared higher and farther than anybody in a gray place dares to dream. It was like some beautiful bird flapped into our drab little cage and made those walls dissolve away, and for the briefest of moments, every last man in Shawshank felt free."

Examples in Myth and Legend

The myths of Lemuria, the lost continent and race, include this early gigantic form of humanity consorting with other life forms evolutionarily behind them. This "mating with the mindless ones" is said to have produced some of the part-human, part-animal creatures immortalized in ancient art and story.

The Pied Piper of Hamlin leads all the rats out of a town by playing his pipes. When the townspeople who hired him refused to pay him, he started playing again and this time the town's children follow along as well.

In India, Tansen is revered as a great musician whose skill caused candles to light and temperatures to rise in the room where he sang incendiary songs.

Flute-playing Kokopelli is a deity of the Southwest American Natives, representative of music and fertility.

Greek Orpheus is said to be a rock star. When he played, the rocks sprouted feet to follow him and keep listening to his amazing music.

Examples in History and Current Events

Troubadours spread the lore of chivalry throughout feudal Europe.

The Renaissance Man or Woman is multi-talented, multi-learned, multi-skilled, and able to converse and write fluently in a number of languages and excel in a number of sports. Science has now explained how music and art contribute to the development of our brains and can make us better in everything else we do. A culture suffers that does not include the arts in education or civil society.

The art of Leonardo Da Vinci, according to the *Da Vinci Code* and *Holy Blood, Holy Grail,* held secret codes about the history and the future of Christianity - that Jesus and Mary Magdalene were married and had a child, whose descendants today still carry the immortal bloodline. Regardless of any hidden meanings, Da Vinci's art is still enjoyed and revered today.

Concerts raise funds to aid specific causes; for instance, Concert for Bangladesh, Willie Nelson's Farm Aid, Live Aid for the Ethiopian famine, Shelter from the Storm for Hurricane Katrina, and Healing in the Heartland for the Oklahoma May 2013 tornado victims.

Singer Taylor Swift has said she can only date men that she can write songs about.

Frida Kahlo and Diego Rivera inspired each other, as well-told in the film *Frida.*

Pablo Picasso was infamous for the number of Muses he had, many of whom overlapped one another's reign.

Architecture is art on a grander scale. It defines cultures and influences people, from pyramids to cathedrals - "the glory that was Greece, and the grandeur that was Rome" - to the intimidating architecture of Nazi Germany with its vast plazas, towering edifices, and 100 foot tall blood-red banners. Across the world today there is a competition to see who can raise the highest skyscraper: Kuala Lumpur has the Petronas Towers, Dubai the Burj Khalifa, and in New York City the always iconic Empire State Building has unfortunately but briefly regained tallest building status in that city.

See more in the BBC series *How Art Made the World.*

Examples in Media

Artists make good characters because they are typically driven, unconventional, troubled, attractive, neurotic, brilliant, and as was said about Lord Byron, he was "Mad, bad, and dangerous to know." What a great story character!

Writer Christian [Ian McGregor] in *Moulin Rouge* is torn between his desire to have his music produced and his secret love for the courtesan Satine [Nicole Kidman]. For a delirious while his two loves mesh; then tragically they do not.

Bio-pics about artists can capture the tenor of a time and give your audience a peek into different worlds. For two diverse artists creating at the same time check out the Cole Porter bio-pic *De-Lovely* and the documentaries and film work of the German director, inventor, and cinematographer Leni Riefenstahl, in particular her *Olympia* and *Triumph of the Will.*

And don't think the writer is a dull artistic character for stories or screen just because they're not dashing around having wild adventures. They can dish up a lot of drama, comedy, and pathos as in *The Last Station* about Russian writer Leo Tolstoy, *Adaptation, Capote,* and *Impromptu* about female author George Sand and her musician lovers and friends.

Music and movies about musicians offer a myriad of perspectives on the inner turmoils and outer troubles as these unconventional people bump heads with society and conformity - "I Walk the Line" by Johnny Cash, "The Devil Goes down to Georgia" by Charlie Daniels, and bluesman Robert Johnson's "Crossroads", also memorably recorded by Eric Clapton.

Music can impel and indicate all the extremes of the human heart. Some examples are Handel's "Messiah", Whitney Houston's "I will always love you", Louis Armstrong's "What a Wonderful World", and the Irish ballad "Danny Boy".

And as the poster for an opera says, "Men cheat, women cry, people die...it's Opera". Some opera characters are indeed artists, such as Wagner's *Meistersinger*, Gluck's *Orfeo ed Euridice*, the starving artists in Puccini's *La Boheme,* and in its modern version, *Rent.*

Other examples of the love of an artist causing drama include:

Van Gogh, Chicago, All That Jazz, Warhol, Intermezzo, Pollock, The Doors, Men in Black III portrays the real-life artist Andy Warhol as an alien

In *Tinker, Tailor, Soldier, Spy* Ann Smiley's lover Bill Hayden brings her a work of art that becomes a minor but important plot point.

Weird Science – a version of the Pygmalion myth

The bio-pics *Hemmingway and Gellhorn* and *Sweet Dreams,* about Patsy Cline.

Examples in Music
"Vincent (Starry Starry Night)" by Don McLean
"Mona Lisa"
"There could never be a portrait of my love."

Symbols
Handprints or circles and dots on a cave wall
Petroglyphs
Murals
Carvings and tools
Paintbrush and palette
Statue half-carved
Masks
Easel, canvas
Museum
Ancient artistic ruins
Musical instruments
Pen and Ink
Typewriter

Keyboard
Piano
Sheets of music
Music stand and empty chair
Drawing pads
Charettes
Blueprints

Key Element – The Shining Action

The Calling – the moment your character takes steps towards deciding what they want to pursue. If you can build in 3 to 5 steps along the way, from an initial slight interest to a fervent desire to pursue it, you can keep raising the tensions for your audience. Throw in resistance all along the way and you will increase the dramatic conflict. This Shining Moment will be the first glimpse of the goal: a statue, a film set, a band.

The Culmination – the victory moment, the eventual attainment of the goal. It could be sculpting and seeing it admired in a museum; making a movie and getting an Oscar; playing an instrument in a band cheered by thousands of fans.

The Object of Desire – this focuses not on the character but on what they have created through their desire. The statue, the book, the Oscar on the mantel, the concert, the band's name in lights....the Groupies.

Written Descriptions

Art is about the exaggeration of reality. It takes something familiar out of its ordinary field of perception and brings it to our attention. It is about presenting what is familiar in an unfamiliar way.

There is a brilliant version of writing about how an artist feels, how they are accepted, or not, by society in Don McLean's "Vincent (Starry Starry Night)".

It's the passion of the artist who does not care what society thinks but creates regardless of society's norms that leads him into conflict with society. Passion by its very definition has no reference to financial gain, which is difficult for those without passion to understand.

Artists are seldom into it for the money and most artists don't make money with their art. It was the same with the early filmmakers and with many still today, particularly the independent filmmakers and those who create web series. Art is for people who are driven to do the art, regardless of its acceptance by society.

No one understood Frank Lloyd Wright when he started out. He was shunned and mocked. Now, he is revered. Like the tragic situation of Vincent Van Gogh, many artists are not appreciated in their own lifetime...more's the pity.

Because we live in a world where money means so much and defines who we are, it is the trial of the artist to maintain their integrity and simultaneously maintain their physical existence.

Give your characters these challenges. Express the drive, the passion, the new idea that separates the artist from the rest of the characters in your story.

It might be Hemingway standing for hours in front of a chest of drawers typing his latest novel.

It might be Michelangelo visiting the marble quarry and choosing the block from which he will carve his next statue.

It could be Monet looking out at his colourful gardens and then recreating them at the palette.

It could be Sibelius out listening to the winds through the pines and the rough sea against the rocky shore of Finland and then turning it into the evocative "Finlandia" symphony.

When the artist is engrossed in their art, they typically take no note of the society around them. Tell us how they are focused and absorbed in the creation of their art – that will tell us that it is a true Love of Art and not just a commercial venture.

Cinematic Techniques

For grand architecture like a Gothic cathedral or pyramids you want to get the feeling of it towering above us. They were designed to be seen from the bottom up, representing the gods holding sway over man. So give us that perspective of looming, impressive and often oppressive power. The same goes for modern skyscrapers.

For a character who is the creator of these edifices (the architect, the pharaoh, the investor), show us their perspective from the top down.

Watch Leni Riefenstahl's *Triumph of the Will* for a superb example on the dynamics of photographing architecture and large spaces.

For paintings and sculpture, travel in and out and/or around the piece itself. The forced perspective of Michelangelo's David presumes that it sits atop a building and is the human version of gigantic public art.

For music, start close on the sheet music or the fingers of the player. Pull out to a wider shot and see how the music affects others. See the "Play it again, Sam" scene in *Casablanca.*

In *The Benny Goodman* story, by shooting from below the elbows up to his face, we see him and the power of the instrument. The camera looking up typically implies that person is more powerful in some way than we who are looking at them.

In *Hemingway and Gellhorn* Ernest writes standing up, with the paper on top of the dresser drawer. We see from the side his arms and hands moving. The oldie-but-goodie shot is the close-up as the typewriter keys move up to hit the page of paper. That's rather dated, but you can see the same concept with keyboards and computers, as well as on cell phones – both the typing in and the readouts. Today's technology plays an important part in the new *Sherlock Holmes* Masterpiece Mystery series.

The opposite POV is the camera standing face-on to the writer as she types out the story. You don't see the type hit the page but you do see the emotions that she feels. The same thing can be done with musicians as we observe the effect their music has on them.

Conclusion
Humans would not be human without art. Make this an integral aspect of at least one of your characters and you can expand your audience reach and recognition.

The arts are wonderfully complex and contradictory worlds within themselves. Placing your characters in those turbulent streams of creativity, power, pride, temptation, defeat, or victory can create compelling dramatic conflicts and resolutions.

*****

Exercise #1 – Awareness
What to you is the most beautiful piece of art, be it painting, music, dance, sculpture, writing, etc.?

*****

Exercise #2 – Writing
Write 2-3 lines of dialogue where one character is trying to explain something to another character. First make one of them an artist and the other one not.

Then rewrite the scene with both characters as artists so they won't have to keep explaining the jargon.

*****

Further Reading
Ada – Vladimir Nabokov
Book of Kells, The – and other illustrated manuscripts
Concerning the Spiritual in Art – Wassily Kandinsky
Fountainhead, The – Ayn Rand
How Ireland Saved Civilization – Thomas Cahill
Idylls of the King – Alfred Lord Tennyson
Inner Drives – Pamela Jaye Smith
Interaction of Color - Joseph Albers
Paleopoetics – Christopher Collins
Picture of Dorian Gray – Oscar Wilde
Point and Line to Plane – Wassily Kandinsky
Power of the Dark Side – Pamela Jaye Smith
Symbols.Images.Codes – Pamela Jaye Smith
White Goddess, The – Robert Graves

Further Viewing
Basquait
Black Swan
(Burden of Dreams), Cave of Forgotten Dreams, Fitzcarraldo
– Werner Herzog (about)
Chorus Line
Fame
Fitzcarraldo
Girl in the Cafe, The
Girl with a Pearl Earring
Glee and *High School Musical*
How Art Made the World – BBC series
La Boheme – Puccini's opera about starving artists in Paris
Mao's Last Dancer
Mister Holland's Opus
Muse, The
New York Stories
Phantom of the Opera, The
Pianist, The
Picture of Dorian Gray, The
Pollack
Power of Myth, The – Joseph Campbell and Bill Moyers

Rent - the modern adaptation of Puccini's *La Boheme*
Searching for Sugar Man – Oscar-winning documentary
Sentinels of Silence
Shakespeare in Love
Slings and Arrows – Canadian series about a Shakespeare company
Soloist, The
Thomas Crown Affair, The – about a playboy art thief and a detective
Xanadu – Olivia Newton-John is a roller-skating muse

Websites   *Masonic World*
http://www.masonicworld.com/education/files/artjan02/marcus/sevenliberalartsandsciences.htm

CHAPTER SEVEN

LOVE OF ADVENTURE

Oh! I have slipped the surly bonds of Earth
And danced the skies on laughter-silvered wings;
Sunward I've climbed, and joined the tumbling mirth
of sun-split clouds, — and done a hundred things
You have not dreamed of — wheeled and soared and swung
High in the sunlit silence. Hov'ring there,
I've chased the shouting wind along, and flung
My eager craft through footless halls of air....

Up, up the long, delirious, burning blue
I've topped the wind-swept heights with easy grace.
Where never lark, or even eagle flew —
And, while with silent, lifting mind I've trod
The high untrespassed sanctity of space,
- Put out my hand, and touched the face of God.

"High Flight"
John Gillespie Magee, Jr.

There's a type of love that scales mountains, moves rivers, and changes worlds. This sort of love often breaks up families, ruins careers, and ends in destitution and death.

Yet it keeps luring people into its web, offering the chance of rewards beyond compare in emotional satisfaction, lifelong relationships, and worldly riches. This love is the Love of Adventure.

Since the first hominids dropped down from the trees to explore the savannahs, we humans have distinguished ourselves by a desire to know what's around the corner, "over the hills and far away", and even beyond the stars.

The Defining Myth
The Odyssey – one of the most popular adventure stories ever. The saga tells of the Greek warrior Odysseus' ten year journey back home to Ithaca from the fall of Troy. Having come up with the Trojan Horse, Odysseus annoyed some of the gods participating in the outcome of that ten year battle between the Greeks and the Trojans. Poseidon in particular used his sea god powers to cast Odysseus and his men hither and yon on foreign shores where they faced all sorts of challenges, loss and rewards.
Read Homer's entire *Iliad* and *Odyssey* to get lots of ideas for stories you can write dealing with these same issues. Some note that the journeys of Odysseus can be aligned with the chakras.

Exemplar Movies
Raiders of the Lost Ark – all four films plus the very good TV series, Young Indiana Jones.

Why it exists (evolutionary back-story)
Given that every human begins as a single fertilized cell and then expands and grows and becomes more complex, there is a deep evolutionary drive to expand and grow. It is how we are created in the first place. Anthropologically, we human primates managed to get our knuckles off the ground some aeons ago and now we are trying to grab the stars.

The search for new resources often compels primitive tribes to explore new lands looking for fresh water, flora and fauna. Thank goodness for the survival of the species that almost every group has a few members driven to explore the wilds. Once the new frontiers are conquered, civilizing forces start moving in. Lots of American Westerns are about this very process: the drive to find new resources for the "tribe" and the tribe moving in and settling down, changing the system where cowboy law had once ruled.

How it works (physiology & psychology)
An explanation from the fine website Science Daily addresses the physiology of the Love of Adventure thusly: "Dopamine is a natural chemical which relays messages in the brain controlling aspects of movement, cognition and behaviour. It helps control the brain's reward and pleasure centres and regulates emotional responses such as fear."
http://www.sciencedaily.com/releases/2011/11/111104102125.htm

Science has identified the biochemistry for risk tolerance, not surprisingly a very strong factor in those we label "adrenalin junkies". There are indeed some people who just crave the thrill. Perhaps you know someone who does or perhaps you yourself like to ride scary roller coasters? Watch horror-suspense movies? White-water raft? Rock climb? Bungee-jump? Do Mixed Martial Arts? Swim with sharks? An understanding of the addictive power of adrenalin and the basic physiology that craves adrenalin will help you write these characters with more insight.

In *Star Trek* the infant James Tiberius Kirk is born in a bath of adrenalin as the starship evacuates. His mom is in labor as his dad dies sacrificing his life to save the crew. What a compelling chemical beginning to a life of adventure.

Sexually speaking, females tend to be drawn to adventurous Alpha Males. For breeding purposes anyway. They also typically settle down and raise families with Beta Males. This tendency is evident in birds and mammals of all sorts, including humans. The premise is that the Alpha Males have healthy adventurous disease-free genes and that's exactly what you want to propagate the species. Unfortunately they do not typically make good mates or fathers and for that you need the Beta Males. It's a system that has worked for millennia to further the survival of many, many species.

Proof in humans is that ten percent of children are fathered by other than their mother's official mate. Think what great story complications you could weave from just this concept.

There is a sense of aloneness and sometimes alienation in the soul of an adventurer because others cannot truly understand them if they are not adventurers themselves.

How it serves us now
Civilizations rise and fall. Much of that is dependent upon local resources such as water, arable soil, plants and animals. When that changes, everything changes. Then the person with the drive for adventure can lead you out of danger and destruction and into a new "promised land". Post-apocalyptic stories have protagonists that are physically and often also emotionally and socially adventurous, as in *The Hunger Games, Road Warrior(s), The Postman, Waterworld,* and *Avatar.*

Currently our planet is suffering from the ravages of "extraction capitalism", which tends to take what it wants regardless of consequences. The consequences of these current actions may one day force us deeper into the earth and the seas, or off-planet in search of new resources. In your stories a protagonist with a sense of adventure might well save the human race.

Examples in Myth and Legend

How many adventure stories begin with the young man or woman setting out to "seek their fortune"? Lots. Remember that in feudal societies it was typical for the first son to inherit the estate. The second son went into the military. The third son joined the Church. The fourth son and any beyond that were pretty much on their own. Typically they went on to seek their fortune in strange lands among exotic people. Sometimes that worked really well. Sometimes they were never heard from again.

The Mesopotamian saga of Gilgamesh and Enkidu is full of adventure as they search for the secret to immortality, battling scorpion men, and diving to the bottom of the sea.

Jason and the Argonauts have nothing but adventure.

The legend of King Solomon's Mines lost somewhere in Africa have drawn adventurers for thousands of years, including in the film *Congo*.

A sense of adventure carried the Maori thousands of miles across the Pacific to Aotearoa, the Land of the Long White Cloud [New Zealand].

The majority of women in mythologies are goddesses, typically the earth mother or lover archetypes...not adventuresses. However there are a few exceptions.

Greco-Roman adventuress Atalanta went on the great Calydonian boar hunt with the guys, was the swiftest runner in the land, and some stories say she accompanied Jason and the Argonauts on the quest for the Golden Fleece.

Artemis/Diana was goddess of the hunt and Lady of Wild Things. Orion was her huntsman for awhile, but he ended up a constellation. In the siege of Troy, Artemis favored the Trojans.

The Norse Valkyries were adventurous warrior virgins who gathered slain heroes from a battlefield and carried them on their horses up to Valhalla, the warrior heaven.

We need more stories of adventurous women...perhaps you will write them.

Examples in History and Current Events
In the 13th century Marco Polo left Italy for the Far East, allegedly traversing the Silk Road, learning about the locals, and bringing back knowledge and goods from China and places between. Regardless of whether he actually made all those journeys, his writings have inspired tens of thousands of people to go on their own adventures.

The Chinese Admiral Zheng He used navigation technology in the 1400s to explore the world beyond the South China Sea. Besides Malaya, Java, Indonesia, and India he was also reputed to have explored Madagascar and the Horn of Africa.

Ferdinand Magellan and Captain Cook sailed from Europe through the Strait of Magellan at the bottom of South America, where the difference between the Atlantic and Pacific Oceans is forty feet, creating dangerous, turbulent waters. Charles Darwin sailed through the Strait on the Beagle, eventually to visit the Galapagos Islands and find further validation for his theory of evolution. President Teddy Roosevelt's Great White Fleet went through on its show-of-power mission. Every voyage from the Atlantic to the Pacific was in those days a great adventure.

Spanish conquistador Hernando Cortez was on a mission from the Catholic God (via the Pope) who sent him to the New World. He burned the boats they came in to ensure his men would stay and fight for the Church, the glory of God, and the gold. Other conquistadors also left their mark, their genes, their language, and their ways in the forever-altered "New World".

Admiral Bird, Robert Falcon Scott, and Ernest Shackleton were polar explorers whose exploits still stir the imagination.

British explorer Captain James Cook, sailing the South Pacific on his ship *Endeavor*, said he wanted to "Go farther than any man has been before me...as far as I think it is possible for a man to go".

Sir Richard Francis Burton located the source of the Nile and translated the *1001 Arabian Nights* for fascinated and scandalized Europeans.

Stephens and Catherwood discovered long-lost cities in Mezo and South America.

Theodore "Teddy" Roosevelt spent a year on safari hunting wild game in Africa and wrote an excellent book about it.

In 1953 Sir Edmund Hilary was the first man to reach the summit of Mount Everest, accompanied by his friend and Sherpa guide, Tenzing Norgay.

Alexandra David Neel was the first white woman into Lhasa, Tibet.

Gertrude Bell – writer, traveler, archaeologist, and spy in the Middle East

Airplane fighter pilots and test pilots break new frontiers, from Charles Lindberg to Amelia Earhart, Chuck Yeager, and the Mercury, Gemini, and Apollo crews who led the way to the moon. From that program came the Space Shuttle, the International Space Station, and continuing exploration into the solar system and beyond.

Some other female explorers and adventurers are:

Harriet Quimby – aviatrix
Freya Stark – explorer, linguist, and designer of propaganda for the British in WWII

Valentina Tereshkova first woman in space
Mary Henrietta Kingsley – explorer
Osa Johnson - explorer, filmmaker
Louise Arner Boyd - Arctic explorer
Isabella Lucy Bird Bishop - first woman elected to Royal
Geographic Society
Grace O'Malley - 16th century Irish pirate
Beryl Markham - aviator/explorer

Doctors without Borders and the Peace Corps -- both are a combination of the desire to do good coupled with a sense of adventure.

"For this is what America is all about. It is the uncrossed desert and the unclimbed ridge. It is the star that is not reached and the harvest sleeping in the unplowed ground., Is our world gone? We say "Farewell." Is a new world coming? We welcome it – and we will bend it to the hopes of man."
Lyndon B. Johnson, U.S. President

Some Hollywood legends were particularly adventurous when it came to racing: James Dean, Steve McQueen (who did his own stunts in the *Bullitt* car chase), and Paul Newman.

Many sports are adventurous – bungee jumping, sky diving, scuba diving, aerobatics, snowboarding, surfing, spelunking, mountain claiming– and engage the extremes of the environment.

Some jobs are by nature adventurous – spying is one that offers all sorts of possibilities for adventure. Special forces troops must be adventurous by nature, and certainly are that by training.

Examples in Media
Adventure stories have been popular since the first tales around the campfire when storytellers recounted such adventures as the great mammoth hunt, the journey of exploration, fighting other tribes or the gods. Some of the greatest adventure stories are the oldest ones such as

Homer's *Iliad* and *Odyssey*, Virgil's *Aeneid*, Dumas' *Three Musketeers,* Cervantes' *Don Quixote,* and J.R.R. Tolkien's *Lord of the Ring* series.

The 2009 *Star Trek* movie offers an excellent example of the Love of Adventure at work in a number of characters, most vividly in that of young James Tiberius Kirk. The first time we see this character (other than as a newborn) he's a cocky ten-year old racing a Corvette across the flat Iowa prairies with a huge space center looming in the background and a motorcycle cop in hot pursuit. The boy runs the 'Vette to the edge of a cliff, bails out, and watches the vintage car somersault into the deep canyon. This visual expression of derring-do sets the tone for Kirk's bravado and his deep desire to race off into the Final Frontier. The rest of the film is full of Jim Kirk adventures.

A line of dialogue that well expresses this Love of Adventure is inherent in all the *Star Trek*s -- "To boldly go where no one has gone before".

Most of the movies of Errol Flynn and Douglas Fairbanks. The *James Bond* films and other spy stories as well. Pirate books and films.

Sarah Connor in the *Terminator* movies and in the *Sarah Connor Chronicles*.

Petra Volare is an 11-year old inventor and adventurer in ancient Crete. The first in the 7-book *Petra Volare* series is *Scroll 1: From the Shadows*; in it Icarus's younger sister creates her own identity and saves her brother.

The award-winning animated film *Up* is another Love of Adventure story that also includes romantic and familial love. Carl, a widowed septuagenarian, and Russell, a young latchkey Wilderness Scout, take an adventure of a lifetime when the widower attaches thousands of helium balloons onto his old house and heads for Paradise Falls in South America, hoping to fulfill his late wife's dream of adventure. Like *Star*

Trek, this movie also has a brief line of dialogue that captures the spirit of most of the characters, from Carl and his wife Ellie, to the boy Russell, the disgraced adventurer-once-hero Muntz, and even to the dog Dug and the bird Kevin -- "Adventure is out there!"

And as Buzz Lightyear of the *Toy Story* series always says, "To infinity and beyond!".

Examples in Music
"Rocket Man" - Elton John
"Space Oddity" - Ground Control to Major Tom
"Secret Agent Man" – Johnny Rivers
The many James Bond films theme songs.

Symbols
The Gear - pickax and pitons, the pith helmet, the wetsuit, the parachute, etc. The balloons in UP are an imaginative and colorful representation of hope, perfect for an animated family film. The fact that they are attached to the century-old home that belonged to Carl and his late wife, is the perfect visual pairing to represent the old man's desire to break free from his grief and to finally fulfill the dream of adventure that he and his wife once shared.

The Leap – launching one's self out into the void is a huge act of faith and adventure. When Butch Cassidy and the Sundance Kid leap off the cliff and into that South American river it takes them away from their old lives and into their new ones. Daredevil Evil Knievel made a career of media adventures and in 2012 Felix Baumgarten set a skydiving record of 128,098 feet up in space down to the earth in 4 minutes and 19 seconds.

The Map or a Globe – shows us the contested territory and how difficult your character's quest will be. Old adventure movies highlight the hero's trail across a map. *Master and Commander* uses this device, as does *Romancing the Stone, Raiders of the Lost Arc,* and *Game of Thrones.* The map is a bigger representation of what you see of your environment and often those who are not on the adventure live it vicariously through the map. And in pirate movies "X" marks the spot.

Key Element – The Shining Action
Include scenes where your adventurous character acquires the right gear and using it signals the start of the adventure. In *Avatar*, Jake Sully mounts the dragon and begins his adventure with the Na'vi. In many stories the dragon, the horse, the aircraft, the automobile are vehicles to carry the protagonist into other territories or alternate universes. Sometimes the device is a word, a wave of a wand, or some magic food -- as when Neo in *Matrix* and *Alice in Wonderland* took the blue pill that hurled them into another world.

Show them going through gateways into a new world – be it leaping off a cliff, going through a doorway, jumping out of an airplane, crossing a border, entering a different environment.

Written Descriptions
From the bottoms of the seas to the surface of Mars and beyond, adventurers explore the unknown, the lost, and the yet-to-be found. A poignant example is Rutger Hauer's dying speech in *Blade Runner*, "I've seen things you people wouldn't believe. Attack ships on fire off the shoulder of Orion. I've watched C-beams glitter in the dark near the Tannhauser Gate. All those moments will be lost in time, like tears in rain. Time to die."

By its very nature a story about the Love of Adventure is big. Wide vistas, far horizons, dangerous heights, gloomy corridors, raucous jungles. The environment is often the object of the protagonist's affections, so its descriptions should be strong and compelling. Using words like "draw in", "vast", "frontier", "vista", "challenge", "breath-taking", "daring", "dangerous", etc. will give your reader a sense of how the characters feel when they are in the settings you describe.

Fill your character's speeches with awe about where they go and what they see. It could be like *Star Trek*'s Far Point Station where you look beyond the edge of the known universe. Alien skyscapes such as two moons, a close planet, different coloured land or flora can all signal an alien environment.

Write about the Key Element: putting on the uniform, leaping off the cliff, making the Leap.

Use shorter and shorter paragraphs and sentences to increase tension.

Use different terms to describe objects on the other side of the gates of adventure. On this side they are trees, on the other side they are sentinels. On this side it is a river, on the other side it is a torrent of fate. On this side a mountain, on the other side a challenge.

Cinematic Techniques
The wide environmental shot. Thelma and Louise driving across the US. The airplane in the sky. The man riding the dragon. The ship tossed on the vast sea. Give us the human in the midst of that which embodies the adventure.

The close tight shot of putting on the uniform, picking up the tools. Taking on the mission, as in *Dances With Wolves*.

Exploring the Environment. The shot in *Lawrence of Arabia* where Lawrence is riding through the desert, stopping at the oasis, and then Sharif riding from the distance up to him. *Waterworld* also has wide shots of the environment that demands adventure. *Cloud Atlas* has some great scenes of characters against the environment, particularly in moments of exploration, as when Tom Hanks and Halle Berry scramble up the steep cliffs.

The Leap. Stepping into the unknown. Jumping out of the airplane. Diving into the ocean.

Start close in on the heroine, zoom out to the whole area affected by her actions. Reverse that.

Jerky camera moves and quick cuts do not necessarily say 'love of adventure'. First you must capture our attention and align us with the heroine's desires. In his exhilarating sports photography, Warren Miller shows us the majesty of the environment and how humans relate to it. He gives us close-ups of the individuals and their personal perspective on what they do. He engages us with their emotions.

Sustained coverage of the huge monstrous processes of nature unfolding before our eyes sucks us into the experience much more effectively than jerky cuts can ever do. The rising tsunami, the encroaching forest fire, the erupting volcano – all deserve long holding shots that make you want to break away and run. It isn't about the character's action so much as it is about the overwhelming environment where the love of adventure takes place.

You could create a montage of Felix Baumgartner jumping from the Red Bull balloon, you cut to Chuck Yeager falling through space trying to get his helmet off, you have base jumpers, bungee jumpers, a diver falling through the waters...it's all about Earth's gravity exerting its pull on us. It can only be expressed by holding the length of the shot.

The love of adventure might well be described as gravity desiring to collect us in its arms.

Conclusion
Love of adventure takes us to other places, opens our minds, moves our hearts.

A story about the Love of Adventure should inspire us to dust off our passports, pack up our pith helmets, and set out for the vast unknown.

Seeing new things, or seeing old things in new ways, is essential for story-tellers.
Certainly for writers, travel is a stimulus to creativity. What we want from creative writers is the imagination to sweep us into new, unexplored realms. Otherwise you are just reporters of the real, documentarians of "what is".

As most of the surface of the earth becomes accessible via on-the-ground travel or Google Earth, the sense of adventure that started humans out on our great migrations tens of thousands of years ago will always draw us to the extremes, the new ones being off-planet, underground, and beneath the surface of the seas.

"Space... the Final Frontier.
These are the voyages of the starship *Enterprise*.
Her ongoing mission: to explore strange new worlds,
to seek out new life forms and new civilizations,
to boldly go where no one has gone before."
Star Trek

*****

Exercise #1 – Awareness
What is the most adventurous thing you have heard of in myth, history, media, real-life...or perhaps even an adventure of your own?

*****
Exercise #2 – Writing
Write a scene where your protagonist is trying to talk a non-adventurer into action but who refuses the challenge. Then write the same scene where the protagonist is talking to a fellow adventurer who accepts the challenge.

*****
Further Reading
Ana Purna, a Woman's Place – Arlene Blum
Art of War, The by Sun Tzu - Samuel B. Griffith
Asian Saga, The – James Clavell
Awakened Warrior, The -Rick Fields, Editor
Book of the Five Rings, The - Miyamoto Musashi / Victor Harris
Clive Cussler adventure novels
Collapse – Jared Diamond
"Dysfunctional Families: Doomed or Divine?" – article by Pamela Jaye Smith
Eastern Approaches – Fitzroy MacLean
Edgar Rice Burroughs – all his works
Eight Feet in the Andes – Durvla Murphy
General George S. Patton, Jr. - books by and about
Heroines - Norma Lorre Goodrich
Inner Drives – Pamela Jaye Smith
Killer Angels, The - Michael Shaara
Leadership and the New Science - Margaret J. Wheatley
Lincoln on Leadership - Donald T. Phillips
Lost World, The – Arthur Conan Doyle
Mars trilogy – Kim Stanley Robinson
Outlander series – Diana Gabaldon
Petra Volare: Scroll 1 From the Shadows – Reece Michaelson and Pamela Jaye Smith
Pippi Longstocking – Astrid Lindgren
Power of the Dark Side, The – Pamela Jaye Smith
Seven Pillars of Wisdom – T.E. Lawrence
Spinsters Abroad: Victorian Lady Explorers – Dea Birkett
Symbols.Images.Codes – Pamela Jaye Smith
Women Warriors, A History - David E. Jones

*****
Further Viewing
20,000 Leagues Under the Sea

21 Balloons	*7 Years in Tibet*
Abyss, The	*Alien vs. Predator*
Around the World in 80 Days	*Babylon Five*
Battlestar Galactica	*Deep Blue, The*
Doctor Who	*Gunga Din*
Happy Feet	*Harriet the Spy*

Incredibles, The
Journey to the Center of the Earth

Lost – TV series	*Lost World, The*
Mountains of the Moon	*Predators*
Princess Bride	*Right Stuff, The*
Star Trek - features and series	*Star Wars* – all

Stargate - features and series
Surfing films: *Chasing Mavericks, Big Wednesday, Endless Summer, Point Break, Blue Crush, Surf Nazis Must Die, etc.*

Swiss Family Robinson	*Toy Story*
Treasure Island	*Under Fire*

Wall-E
Warren Miller's sports movies
        http://www.skinet.com/warrenmiller/videos/warren-millers-flow-state-teaser
Young Indian Jones – TV series

*****
Web links
Alpha Babe Academy   http://alphababeacademy.com/

China Exploration and Research Society
http://www.cers.org.hk

First Earth Battalion   http://www.firstearthbattalion.com/

Joseph Campbell Foundation   www.jcf.org

Institute of Noetic Sciences   www.noetic.org

MYTHWORKS   www.mythworks.net

CHAPTER EIGHT

LOVE OF DEATH & DESTRUCTION

Mankind is composed of two sorts of men –
those who love and create,
and those who hate and destroy.

Jose Marti

Life is a mystery because of death. Life springs up from seeming nothingness, thrives, and then returns to seeming nothingness.

Life is precariously fragile yet also stubbornly persistent. People have survived rebar rods into their brains and signposts completely through the chest. Yet swallow the wrong way or slip on a pickle at the burger joint and it's all over.

From the individual human to the seasons of the year, to the existence of an entire species to the birth and death of stars, and even to the whole of the universe itself -- death comes to all forms. Substance, however, has more longevity: just think of melting down metal to make something new. Same substance, different form.

Our fascination with death and destruction may just be part of our fascination with existence itself. The drive to know how things work, the desire to change things to our will, and the desire to control things can lead to willful acts of death and destruction.

For stories with any of that in them, it is important for you to give us characters and situations that make sense psychologically and philosophically, as well as plot-wise. The more we understand, the more we can write engaging characters and stories – especially on the Dark Side with deadly antagonists.

The Defining Myths
Shiva is the Hindu god of destruction and transformation. After all, if you want an omelet you have to break some eggs. If you want a new world you have to destroy and deconstruct the old one. When Shiva dances the world is destroyed. No coincidence that some weapons have been named Shiva, including a giant laser at the Lawrence Livermore National Laboratory.

Kali is the Hindu goddess of death and time. She carries a bloody scythe and wears a necklace of gore-dripping human heads as she tramples on a mere mortal.

Both these deities have other attributes as well, signifying that death and destruction are also essential for change and growth, for transformation and transfiguration.

J. Robert Oppenheimer, "father of the atomic bomb" said about it, quoting from the Hindu *Bhagavad-Gita*, "If the radiance of a thousand suns were to burst at once into the sky, that would be like the splendour of the mighty one.,.. " He also later quoted, perhaps in warning and perhaps in regret, from the *Gitas*, "I am become Death, the destroyer of worlds".

Exemplar Movie
Heath Ledger's Joker in *The Dark Knight*.

Why it exists (evolutionary back-story)

Life is cyclic. Birth, growth, death, decay. Any observation of life quickly reveals death and decay as part of the process. Just as some astrological signs are aligned with death and endings, so too do cultures large enough for division of labor assign some people the task of dealing with the dead, sometimes just physically or spiritually, sometimes both together. After all, you can't just leave dead bodies lying around. Those specialists typically learned a lot about anatomy that could help the tribe in other ways. Today we call those specialists coroners and medical examiners and have entire TV series about them.

Blood lust is a survival instinct that can overcome all sense of reason during a fight-to-the-death. A throwback to our animal nature, it can be a dramatic and really scary character moment as the body just takes over and does what it does, regardless. This is often called going "berserk" or running "amok".

Genocide may be a holdover from very early days when a village's immune system was vulnerable to strangers. Just look what happened to the inhabitants of the Americas and the Pacific Islands when disease-bearing Europeans arrived on their shores. Anyone seen as "other" posed a real danger to one's own people so eliminating them was a means of survival, not just a hot fit of pique or cold vengeance. History and current events show us that this evolutionary survival tool can get really out of hand – one of those cases of an evil being a "good that was held onto too long".

How it works (physiology & psychology)
Being able to destroy other life lends a sense of godly powers.
Some people just like to break things and kill people.
Sociopaths and psychopaths are this way, even if the results
of their actions isn't always physical death and destruction.
You can get an awfully lot of drama out of one character
emotional destroying another. The term "gaslighting" comes
from the movie *Gaslight* where a husband tries to drive his
new wife crazy by making her think things are happening
which are not.

There's a word for the glee we can feel when others fail,
Schadenfreude. How much of it is simple envy and how much
our fascination with dissolution is a question that can propel
character conflict and character arcs.
Some say that some people who do evil think they are actually
doing good, as in *Star Trek Into Darkness* when Khan kills
thousands to save his 72 colleagues. Yet, it's obvious just
from experience and observation that sometimes people
actually like doing evil, and sometimes people get
inadvertently sucked into the swirl of darkness. See the book
The Power of the Dark Side, in particular the chapter "Lure of
the Dark Side". In *Lawrence of Arabia* there is a scene where
T.E. Lawrence admits over gin and tonics at the officers' club
that what troubled him about having had to execute a
wayward man to keep the tribe together was that he had
enjoyed it.

The challenge in portraying sociopaths and psychopaths is
that they truly are not like other people. Some wiring in their
brain never got hooked up and they simply do not have the
capability of feeling empathy. Appealing to their sense of
justice or consideration for others won't work. Oh, they may
fake it, but watch out – it'll come to no good.

A person's attitude towards death depends greatly upon their belief about life after death. This belief affects their actions, from suicide bombing in order to gain entry into Paradise, to sacrificing themselves in moments of great danger so that others may live. Saints and martyrs willingly embrace death as proof and defense of their faith and in the "sure and certain hope of resurrection".

Dr. Sigmund Freud proposed that the death wish was about returning to the formless void, an echo of Buddhism and some agnostic and atheistic opinions.

The duality of an individual's attitude and approach towards existence has often been cast in the light of two Greek gods – Apollo the god of light, music and medicine and Dionysus the god of wine, 'ecstatic joy, and savage brutality'. Western European thought was greatly influenced by this concept of duality.

And then there's necrophilia, sexual attraction to corpses. These days that probably extends to include zombie-love-sex. Eeewww.

How it serves us now
Unfortunately, particularly in Western cultures, death is seen as the enemy to be avoided at all costs, whereas in many other cultures it is simply part of the natural cycle of existence. Yet even if the culture is accepting and embracing of death and decay the individual usually quails at the thought of being-no-more.

The success of most religions may well lie in their ability to comfort humans confronted with the surety of personal death and extinction by offering the illusion of immortality in some form or fashion.

Some stories posit that extinction is Mother Nature's way of cleaning house. The urge to kill or destroy is just our human way of playing out the nature of life itself on a more personal basis. After all, with 5 Great Extinctions to the history of life on Earth, the 4 Horsemen of the Apocalypse, world-sweeping plagues, and the looming threats of nuclear destruction and climate change there is a lot of death and destruction going on all the time. Finding one's balance of sanity amidst all this – or not finding it – makes for compelling stories.

Examples in Myth and Legend
Most mythic systems have gods and/or goddesses of death. They're not always scary, either. Sometimes they are the comforting arms of surcease from pain and the travails of earthly existence.

Thanatos is the Greek god of death, Hades is the king of the underworld, and Persephone is his lovely queen who spends six months of the year down with him (winter) and then six months up above (summer) with her mother, the vegetation goddess Demeter.

The Greek Atriedes family was cursed from generation to generation and it often out-pictured as death, from chopping up two little boys and feeding them to their father to Clytemnestra slaying her husband King Menelaus in the bathtub right after his return from Troy.

A celebration honouring the dead is a yearly event in many societies. Mexico's Dia de los Muertos [Day of the Dead], Halloween, All Soul's Day, and the Chinese Festival of the Hungry Ghosts are but a few. These could be symbolic backgrounds for your scenes dealing with death and destruction or someone's desire for same.

The Greek war god Ares in the *Xena: Warrior Princess* TV series just loved destruction and death. He was also quite attractive. Thor in Nordic myths is a war god whose hammer Mjolnir brings destruction and death, but always for the cause of the just and good. As anyone familiar with the myths or the recent *Thor* movies knows, Loki is the really bad guy devoted to destruction and to making everyone as miserable as he is. Greek again, Pallas Athena is the goddess of war, wisdom, and civilization.

Just as most spiritual traditions promise resurrection and life eternal or reincarnation and life eternal, many embody this concept in a unique individual, often a god. The returning king or god is a theme throughout myth and legend; the Mezo-American Quetzalcoatl, the Christian Jesus Christ, the Mesopotamian Dammuz, the Norse Baldur, and the Briton's King Arthur.

Examples in History and Current Events
Natural disasters provide plenty of death and destruction. Volcanic eruptions, floods, fires, earthquakes, tsunamis...and in Los Angeles we add riots and celebrity trials.

Some historians think the ball courts in Mezo-America hosted games where the winners, rather than the losers, were sacrificed to the gods...a real honour, that. And perhaps all those blood-drenched pyramids where beating hearts were ripped out as food for the gods was just a misunderstanding of their version of "lift up your hearts unto god".

Thuggees in India were devotees of the death-destruction goddess Kali. They also happened to be blood-thirsty murderers.

Big game hunting isn't as rampant as it used to be, but people still go for the thrill of the chase. Talk with a hunter for some insights into that pursuit of prey and the bringing of death. Films along this line are the *Predator* series, *Running Man*, and *The Hunger Games,* and *The Most Dangerous Game.*

Gladiators in the Roman Coliseum, World Wrestling Foundation and Mixed Martial Arts in the ring, NASCAR explosions-in-waiting whizzing around a track – the promise of destruction and possible death draws thousands in person and millions via media.

Still mostly underground but still happening are to-the-death contests, sometimes pure blood sport and sometimes to resolve gang disputes mano-e-mano.

Goths and Death Metal glamourize the affinity for death and destruction.

Female genital mutilation is a destruction of life force physically and emotionally.

Witch hunts and inquisitions thrive on the deep-seated human drive for destruction of the "other" and blood-lust can quickly infest a group. Ethnic cleansing may not be far away.

Youthful bullies and Mean Girl cliques typically do not belong in this category. Bullies tend to act defensively, triggered by being bullied at home. Cliques are enforcing hierarchies inherent in any animal group. Most child soldiers do not belong here either; they are forced into killing by factors beyond their control who may actually be people who love Death and Destruction.

Some people love violence but it doesn't necessarily mean they love death and destruction. A football player, a boxer, or a soldier may relish violence more as a contact sport without intending death or destruction. For the lover of death and destruction, violence is just one means to an end.

Examples in Media
All the horror, slasher, vampire, zombie, monster, evil alien, ghost, grinder, et cetera stories.

Shakespeare's *Titus Andronicus* is a blood-bath. See the 1999 film *Titus* directed by Julie Taymor.

Detective stories and murder mysteries are sometimes about one-off crimes of passion and sometimes about putting one over on "The Man" again and again just for the thrill.

Post-apocalyptic movies can be cautionary tales about what survivors might do after the destruction and death.

First-person shooter games let us play out our aggressive drives, hopefully without real-world consequences.

The twin vigilantes in *Boondock Saints* are indeed taking out really bad guys who do horrid things, but these good Catholic boys do tend to get swept up into the destruction and the death and go at it with real enthusiasm.

The Walkin' Dude in Stephen King's book *The Stand*.

All of Quentin Tarantino's movies have some characters in them who are in love with death and destruction.

In the *Battle of the Bulge* a German soldier asks his officer (Robert Shaw), when the war will be over? Shaw replies, "The best thing possible is happening. The war will go on.... Indefinitely. On, and on, and on!"

In *Apocalypse Now*, Colonel Kilgore muses, "Someday this war'll be over" with a disappointed look on his face. And then his oft-quoted line, "I love the smell of napalm in the morning. It smells like...victory".

Why would you have a [*Star Wars*] Death Star if you didn't want to destroy everything? The planet-killer weapons of the *Babylon 5* sci-fi series do just that.

In *The Chronicles of Riddick* the Necromongers destroyed everything with glee, gusto, and determination.

The cloaked figure of Death in *The Seventh Seal* plays chess with a mortal. The image of the two of them at the chessboard has been repeated in *Bill and Ted's Excellent Adventure* and *(500) Days* of Summer.

In *The Lion King* the head of the pride advises his little cub about death and destruction with, "It's the Circle of Life, Simba".

The Lord of the Rings pits the lords and hordes of death-and-destruction against the wizards and warriors of the Light.

The Joker in *The Dark Knight* and Silva (Javier Bardem) in *Skyfall*.

Examples in Music
"Alice's Restaurant" – Arlo Guthrie
"Eve of Destruction" – P.F. Sloane
"Senator's Son" – Credence Clearwater Revival
"This is the End" – the Doors
"War, huh, yeah, what is it good for?" – Edwin Starr

Symbols
Skull
Mushroom cloud of nuclear bomb
Radiation sign
Fangs
Sword
Hangman's noose
Grave
Ghosts
Fire
Blood
Bones
Shattered things
Decayed flowers
Moldy food
Skull & crossbones

Key Element – The Shining Action
The poised moment between wholeness and destruction, between life and death. That moment between the outbreath and the inbreath when all possibilities exist. It can be as impersonal as the drone-driver's finger hovering over the "fire" button and the quiet village thousands of miles away about to be obliterated. It can be as personal as two people sword-fighting and one getting and then pressing their advantage to the death.

Show it as a long timeless moment of choice and you will strengthen both what came before and what comes after. In *Saving Private Ryan* the interpreter who was chosen to go on the mission lobbies to let a captive German go, instead of being killed by the other soldiers. Later, the German comes back and knifes to death one of the American soldiers. The interpreter, in his anger and guilt, picks up a rifle and shoots the German.

It will instill the possibility of a moral dilemma you can play up in your story. Or the lack of it, which can be disturbingly effective, as in Tarentino's *Inglorious Basterds*.

Written Descriptions
Snakes in Suits: When Psychopaths Go To Work is an excellent analysis of how sociopaths and psychopaths who love destruction and death go about deceiving others, weaving their hypnotic spell, getting their way, and then dumping the people who were supposedly their friends, lovers, trusted colleagues. It provides a veritable outline for this character and even includes suggestions on how to recognize, fend off, or counteract their actions. If you are writing about this type of person, do use this reference book.

Spend plenty of time describing what a character who loves destruction sees. Where others might see a hollowed-out shell of a bombed out building, your character could see the "empty rib-cage of a formerly alive and breathing creature"; where ordinary people might turn up their noses at the stink of a rotting corpse, this character could be exhilarated by "the sweet smell of decay".

They may be fascinated by the dismantling of a thing, a personality, a body – so describe for us that fascination, the looks, the touch, the feel, etc. The arsonist is always fascinated with the fire.

Steep yourself in Clive Barker, Stephen King, and *The Silence of the Lambs* series for some excellent examples of this kind of love.

When a person flips into their destructive mode and goes berserk from bloodlust, change the way you write about them and how they speak. Use short abrupt sentences, or just inarticulate yells like in many battle scenes.

Sometimes the soft-spoken controlled dialogue is more horrifying than shrieking threats of mayhem. When Thulsa Doom (James Earl Jones) says in *Conan The Barbarian* "They shall all drown in lakes of blood", there is no doubt whatsoever that this guy loves death and destruction.

Characters working from this type of love usually have a real sense of confidence. They are quite convinced that they are right in what they are doing, be it pulling the wings off a fly or genocide on a mass scale. So, they will not have those heart-searching moments of choice, despair, or regret. They may even speak and act cheerfully about what they are doing because it totally fits their worldview.

Cinematic Techniques
Close-up on the torturous or killing cut. Blood and guts.

The reaction shot of the person doing the killing, to see the Love of Death and Destruction on their face.

Reverse angle to show what the victim sees: the bullet or arrow headed in their direction, the blade or missile coming down, etc.

This subject lends itself well to metaphors. Stepping out of the flames can represent the villain's devilish mission or the hero's escape from the fires of hell. For the former see Willem Dafoe's Raven in *Streets of Fire,* Thulsa Doom in *Conan the Barbarian*, and *The Terminator*. For the latter see *Indiana Jones and the Temple of Doom* and the cleansing fires at the end of *Apocalypse Now*, when the hero Captain Willard leaves Colonel Kurtz's festering compound of death and destruction.

People circled round and watching with lust for violence in their eyes: cage fighting, sword fighting, cock or dog fights. See *Fight Club, Raging Bull,* and *The Fighter* for some great examples. The thrill of some contests, like the drinking contest in Tibet at the opening of *Raiders of the Lost Ark*, where Miriam out drinks the local bruiser to everyone's rhythmic cheers. Then thanks to the pursuing Nazis, that place goes up in flames, propelling the Protagonists onto the next step of their adventures. Show us the elements and the people's use of and reaction to them: fists, ropes, liquor bottles, etc.

The quiescent results of someone's Love of Death and Destruction: in *Apocalypse Now*, moving up-river into Colonel Kurtz's compound with its severed heads and rotting corpses. Lines of crucified bodies as in *Spartacus* or *The Life of Brian*; the Romans could have just exiled those people, but instead they tortured them to death.

And it's not all just fast cuts. Certainly the frenzied action of battle lends itself to quick cuts. But for the *coup de gras*, that death cut needs lingering finesse as we watch the victim realize they're about to die. Time slows down for a person in a life-threatening situation so show us that achingly slow progression towards the tragic end.

Live by the sword, die by the sword. It's quite satisfying to see the lover of Death and Destruction brought down by the very thing they planned to use against others. In *Raiders of the Lost Ark* we are first horrified and then we cheer when the evil Nazi's face melts after the Lost Arc is opened. Similarly, you want to show us the expression of gleeful anticipation, the item itself, and then the shock, awe, and horror as he realizes his plan has turned against him.

Conclusion

Since all life must eventually face death, you will always have a connection with your audience when this is an essential part of a character or a story.

Be sure to make it increasingly clear whether your character is motivated by rage, madness, grief, or just plain morbidity.

The love of death and destruction creates great characters and dangerous situations – just the thing for your protagonists to overcome.

*****

Exercise #1 – Awareness

What is the most destructive person or event you can think of from myth, history, current events, or media?

*****

Exercise #2 – Writing

Write a short scene where one person does not want to destroy or kill but is urged to do so by someone else in order to save the day, save other people, etc.

Then re-write the scene where that same person is quite ready to do the destruction and the killing and have the other person trying to convince them not to.

****

Further Reading
1491 – The Americas Before Columbus – Charles C. Mann
Beyond the Pleasure Principle – Sigmund Freud
Decameron, The – Boccaccio
"Dirge without Music" [poem] - Edna St. Vincent Millay
Golden Compass, The trilogy – Philip Pullman
Inner Drives – Pamela Jaye Smith
Life Against Death – Norman O. Brown
Picture of Dorian Gray – Oscar Wilde
Power of the Dark Side, The - Pamela Jaye Smith
Silence of the Lambs, The series
Snakes in Suits: When Psychopaths go to Work – Babiak & Hare
Symbols.Images.Codes - Pamela Jaye Smith
Under the Volcano – Malcolm Lowry
"War – huh! What is it good for?" – article by Pamela Jaye Smith

Further Viewing
Addams Family, The
Battle of the Bulge –"When will the war be over?" "It's the best of all possible endings, the war will continue forever and ever."
Beyond Honor
Boondock Saints
Conan the Barbarian
Dark Knight, The
Death Takes a Holiday
Dexter
Dr. Strangelove
Fight Club
Friday the 13TH – the series
Girl with the Dragon Tattoo, The – entire series of books and films
Gladiator
Hotel Rwanda
Hunger Games, The
Indiana Jones and the Temple of Doom
James Bond films – all those big bad guys out to destroy the world

Javier Bardem characters in *No Country for Old Men* and *Skyfall*
Killing, The
Killing Fields, The
Mad Max – the series of films
Meet Joe Black
Mummy, The - series of films
Night of the Living Dead
Nightmare on Elm Street, A – series of films
Predator
Quentin Tarentino – all of his movies have characters in them who are in love with death and destruction.
Saga of Bjorn, The - animated short
http://www.youtube.com/watch?v=MV5w262XvCU
Silence of the Lambs, The - series of films
Spawn
Zombie Apocalypse

J. Robert Oppenheimer
http://www.history.com/speeches/speeches-j-robert-oppenheimer-on-government-secrecy#speeches-j-robert-oppenheimer-on-government-secrecy

CHAPTER NINE

INTERSPECIES LOVE

A SUDDEN blow: the great wings beating still
Above the staggering girl, her thighs caressed
By the dark webs, her nape caught in his bill,
He holds her helpless breast upon his breast.
How can those terrified vague fingers push
The feathered glory from her loosening thighs?
And how can body, laid in that white rush,
But feel the strange heart beating where it lies?

"Leda and the Swan"
William Butler Yeats

With so much romance, love, lust, and just plain sex going on between humans and vampires, humans and werewolves, humans and zombies, and humans and who-knows-what, let us first define Interspecies Love.

If the human is mating with anyone that is now or ever was an actual human who has been compromised by a DNA override such as a curse, a bite, the phase of the moon, etc., that is not Interspecies.

Some creatures are on the borderline between human and non-human, such as fairies, elves, and gnomes, depending on the mythology and the story. In *The Lord of the Rings* for instance, all these races were humanoid and therefore their love affairs were not inter-species but intra-species.

In mythology there are myriad examples of humans mating with animals, angels, and deities. A modern version is Wim Wenders' *Wings of Desire*, where an angel falls in love with a human and gives up his angelic form to become human in order to be with her.

You might suppose all aliens would fit the bill. But not all off-planet beings would qualify. Some are still quite human, such as Leeloo in *The 5TH Element*, who has four times the DNA of Earthly humans. She's just more human than humans, rather than being of a separate species. The *Star Trek* series is filled with lots of alien - but humanoid - beings [Romulan, Vulcan, Klingon, etc.] who mate with humans just fine – as Captain Kirk proves again and again.

Interspecies Love is an excellent story device through which to make observations on and suggestions for the way we humans treat each other, both as individuals and as societies, nations, and races. It is also a clever way to portray the more animal-like aspects of our human nature.

The Defining Myth
"...the sons of God saw the daughters of men that they were fair; and they took them wives of all which they chose....There were giants in the earth in those days; and also after that, when the sons of God came in unto the daughters of men, and they bare children to them, the same became mighty men which were of old, men of renown." *Genesis 6: 2 & 4*

Ancient astronaut aficionados frequently quote these verses as proof that this planet was visited by aliens. Between this and the angels they do have a curious case.

Exemplar Movie
Avatar

Why it exists (evolutionary back story)

There comes a time in the progress of evolution when increasingly complex diversity requires a new taxonomy. At that point there is a separation of the species and interbreeding is no longer possible. If it were then all creatures might just be a huge muddle of mixed-up genes and who knows what you'd end up with – which has inspired a number of stories such as *The Island of Dr. Moreau* and the Jessica Alba TV series *Dark Angel* where she is part-feline. These stories are not such a far cry these days when we're putting chicken genes into tomatoes and spider genes into milk cows. Who knows what might have happened had Nature not laid down lines over which the genes cannot naturally cross.

Until fairly recently it was thought that early humanoids such as the Cro-Magnon and the Neanderthals did not interbreed either with each other or with homo sapiens sapiens (us). New evidence reveals that we all did. You probably won't be too surprised to learn that many humans have Neanderthal genes. Jean Auel's *The Clan of the Cave Bear* series posited this interbreeding and the breaking away of the different groups to pursue their own track, leaving the older types to fade into pre-history.

Some imaginative versions of humanity's source calls for off-world aliens doing genetic manipulation on the local primates to create modern humans. Depending on the nature of those aliens this could be Interspecies. But if you watch *Stargate*, the last episodes of *Battlestar Galactica*, or read Douglas Adams' *The Hitchhiker's Guide to the Galaxy*, you find a feedback loop of humanoid-to-humanoid.

How it works (physiology & psychology)

If you ascribe to the idea that genes have their own agenda and are always searching for fresh DNA and stronger immune systems, then surely some humans have at times looked upon favoured animals and said, "Yes, let's be more like that!" Typically though they tended to eat the hearts and body parts of the creatures rather than mate with them. Lying down with a lion doesn't have quite the appeal of slow-roasted lion heart. But you can see how the stories would be spun around the hunter's campfires.

Parallel with and opposite to the physical drive to enrich the local gene pool is the psychological drive to keep it pure. A persistent tendency among invading peoples is to categorize the people they invade as "not quite human". They are animalistic, heathens, pagan, primitive, and not worthy of being treated like humans. There is also a tendency for the invading males to mate with the invadee females. It seldom goes the other way. And you seldom hear anyone pointing out that if the locals are "not really human" then is your mating with them bestiality?

How it serves us now

Is this preparing us for alien contact? Is it an artifact of ancient astronauts doing breeding experiments here on Earth? What is the truth behind the longevity and strength of this concept? It is a long-lived tendency as evidenced in cave paintings, in hieroglyphics on Egyptian temple friezes, sculpted on Mayan pyramids, and preserved in the folklore of cultures around the world.

The concept is still used to justify people's maltreatment of other humans because they are "not like us". Genocide is just a short step away.

Dirty jokes abound about people having sex with non-human species, particularly farm animals.

And really, you've just got to ask...what's the deal with alien anal probes?

Examples in Myth and Legend

Sphinxes, griffins, centaurs, gorgons, Anubis and other such Egyptian gods, mermaids.... With so many part human/part animal creatures in the myths of the world one begins to wonder if there might not have been some facts behind the stories. Is it racial memory, the preservation of deep history in myth, the fanciful telling of science experiments gone bad? Or perhaps a misunderstanding of the complexity of evolution and the branching of the tree of life from single-cell life forms to today's humans? Many very interesting, fun, exciting, inspiring, or scary stories center around some mix of humans and another species.

Greek king god Zeus was a rampant womanizer of mortal females, immortal females, and half-mix females. Seduction was often easy because, well, he was king of the gods. Often though, the mortal girls knew about his goddess-wife Hera's jealous rages and preferred not to be turned into a cow. Zeus disguised himself for many of his affairs. As a bull, he kidnapped young Europa. As a swan, he seduced Leda, who bore him Pullox and Helen (later of Troy).

In a similar case of bird-to-human mating Christianity portrays the divine Holy Spirit as a dove, visiting the mortal virgin Mary – the result being Jesus.

In Cretan myths Pasiphae was the wife of King Minos. Minos was given a white bull that he was supposed to sacrifice to the gods. He treasured it and didn't sacrifice it. The angry god caused his wife Queen Pasiphae to fall in love with the bull and mate with it, using a device created by Daedalus. The result was the half-human half-bull Minotaur. Daedalus then built the labyrinth in which the Minotaur was imprisoned.

Joseph Campbell tells the tale of a native American princess who marries a buffalo god to help save her people.

Oscar Wilde's "The Fisherman and the Mermaid" in his *Fairy Tales* book is a version of the Irish stories about selkies, as in *The Secret of Roan Inish*. Selkies are seals who come to shore, shed their skin and take on the appearance of human women. Hide the skin and she stays human; if she puts it back on she returns to being a seal.

Examples in History and Current Events
A wicked rumour was put out about Catherine the Great that she died when a beloved horse weighed too much for the harness holding it above her bed and it crashed down, killing them both. Serious historians wave this off but the Czarina was however known to have lots and lots and lots of very human lovers.

These sorts of accusations and aspersions are always being cast about, particularly about people who handle animals.

And as above, this concept is too often used to oppress other people by categorizing them as animals.

Though we have no real-life cases at this point, hundreds or thousands of years from now there might be plenty of examples of human earthlings mating with off-world species. It can certainly make for intriguing sci-fi, fantasy, and supernatural stories.

Examples in Media
His Monkey Wife by John Collier is an amusing and pointed allegory for miscegenation. In this book an Englishman comes back from Africa with an astonishingly literate female chimpanzee who is in love with him. [Collier also wrote the screenplay for the Hepburn-Bogart film, *The African Queen*.]

Avatar is an excellent example of technologically advanced cultures taking advantage of other beings who are seen as "less than". There is interspecies romantic Love between Jake and Neytiri and a generalized mutual respect and love between the human scientist Grace and the Na'vi.

In *The Little Mermaid* a fish-girl gives up her voice in order to get legs and be able to walk on land and marry the prince.

The first *Alien* film shows female human crew-member Lambert being brutally and fatally raped by the Alien. Earlier, the male crewman Kane was orally raped and in the grossest case of interspecies breeding ever, gives birth to the new alien as it bursts out of his chest.

In *Babylon 5* one of the aliens had "multiple sexual appendages" which others found fascinating, not scary.

Examples in Music
"Earth Girls are Easy" - Julie Brown
"The Man Who Fell to Earth"

Symbols
Two very different versions of the same thing in juxtaposition: eyes, hands, sex organs, etc.

In *Avatar* the helicopters and the flying dragons well represent the differences between the humans and the Na'vi.

Mixed creatures such as centaurs, sphinxes, mermaids, etc.

Key Element – The Shining Action
The kiss and the transformation because of it - like frogs turning back into princes. There is the look of wonderment [*Starman*] or the look of astonished terror [*Alien*].

In *Galaxy Quest* when human Fred Kwan and Thermian Laliari embrace, her "appearance generator" is over-ridden by her true form and an octopus tentacle comes up behind Fred and wraps him in an embrace. She gives him a questioning look that says, "You okay with this?" He swoons into her arms, both humanoid and octopoid.

The actual mating act, as with Leda and the swan [Zeus] from the Pompeii mural.

The birth of the offspring with characteristics of both parents' species, as in *Rosemary's Baby*.

Written Descriptions
Alien species can be the metaphor for human groups and conflicts between them. In *District 9* the sharp delineations of white-vs.-black apartheid were played out with the humans-vs.-aliens. In *Alien Nation* the Newcomers were stand-ins for issues of racism, immigration, gender discrimination, and sexual orientation. The book series *Sparrow* by Mary Doria Russell and *The Golden Torque* series by Julian May both offer deep commentary on human customs, myths, religions, and prejudices through the use of interspecies interactions.

Compare and contrast – how are their heads-limbs-mouths-sex organs alike or different? Make the descriptions either wondrous or horrifying, depending on the nature of the impending relationship between the human and the alien.

Show the differences before you get them together. Laliari in *Galaxy Quest*; when they forget to turn on their Appearance Generators, the earthlings see the Thermians in their true form of tall, upright walking octopi not even faintly resembling humans. In *Starman* the ball of light took on the form of Jeff Bridges by absorbing his DNA through a lock of hair. It's still an alien, it just looks human. The alien and the earth woman make love and she is impregnated with the seed of her cloned late husband.

If positive results -- a stronger bond to something higher and different.

If negative results – unfortunate, dreadful, or deadly. It could be widespread enough to become an extinction-level event.

Be clear about the purpose of the point of contact. In *Star Trek* Kirk going after the alien chicks reveals his character and creates character arcs. In *Alien* the 'mating' is a story arc and drives the plot forward.

Cinematic Techniques
Galaxy Quest – Tech Sergeant Chen [Fred Kwan] [[Tony Shalloub]] is about to embrace the Thermian Laliari. We can only see them from the waist up and she still appears human. Then her octopus arms come up to embrace him and it's really obvious that they are very different from one another. She gives him a questioning look, he shrugs in love's delight, and they fall into a passionate kiss. To emphasize the alien nature of it, Guy Fleegman [Sam Rockwell] makes a face and says, "Ooooh, that's not right!"

When bringing together different species you want to photograph them face-to-face from the same angle if it is a mutually accepting situation. If it is predatory in any way then the predator is at the higher angle looking down on and overpowering the prey. A most unsettling example is the alien attack on Lambert [Veronica Cartwright] in the first *Alien* film. We do not see an actual rape but it is strongly implied.

Show the non-human's point of view of humans, like in *Predator*, when we saw through the alien's infra-red vision. Or if there is a compound eye, you see multiple images. You could even have a character who looks like (and is played by) a human. Give them odd-looking eyes via contact lenses and when you show their point of view, have it significantly different from human vision – aha! they're an alien.

Conclusion
Be clear on the purpose of the point of contact. In *Star Trek* Captain Kirk continually going after the alien chicks reveals his character, the character of those commenting on it, and creates character arcs. In *Alien* both horrifying rapes are part of the story arc, intensify the horror, and drive the scary plot forward.

Be sure to give us the follow-up. If positive results – a stronger bond to something higher and different for one or both characters, and as in *Avatar*, for a wider group. If negative results – show us how unfortunate, dreadful, or deadly it is and how far that effect reaches, as in *Alien*(s).

Interspecies Love is a really rich situation you can use to make all sorts of statements and send all sorts of messages in your stories – while greatly entertaining us in either heart-warming or terrifying ways.

*****

Exercise #1 – Awareness
What is the most unique mating between species you have come across (presumably in myth or media)?

*****

Exercise #2 – Writing
Write a scene where interspecies love/sex takes place. It can be either terrifying and oppressive or tender and loving. In your descriptions and dialogue compare and contrast the two beings: how are their heads/limbs/mouths/sex organs alike or different?

****

Further Reading
Aesop's Fables - Laura Gibbs
Bhagavad-Gita, Mahabharata, Rig Veda, Upanishads - Hindu classics
Bible, The
Bimi - Rudyard Kipling
Bulfinch's Mythology
Faerie – Brian & Wendy Froud
Golden Bough, The - Sir James Frazer
Greek Myths, The - Robert Graves
Grimm's Fairy Tales - the Brothers Grimm
Inner Drives – Pamela Jaye Smith
Joseph Campbell...... All his works. In particular:
      The Power of Myth - from the Bill Moyers TV show
      Hero with a Thousand Faces (aka the Hero's Journey)
      Inner Reaches of Outer Space, Metaphor as Myth & Religion
      The Masks of God - mythology through time
Library of the World's Myths and Legends - Peter Bedrick Books

Metamorphosis - Virgil, Roman poet and mythologist
Mother Goose - compilations of folklore and fairy tales
Mythic Past, The - Thomas Thompson [on the myths of the Bible]
Mythologies (of many cultures, separate books) - Geoffrey Parrinder
Mythology - Edith Hamilton
New Larousse Encyclopedia of Mythology
Painted Bird, The - Jerzy Kozinski
Power of the Dark Side, The – Pamela Jaye Smith
Stranger in a Strange Land – Robert A. Heinlein
Swallow, The & *Children of God* – Mary Doria Russell
Symbols.Images.Codes – Pamela Jaye Smith
Woman's Dictionary of Symbols & Sacred Objects – Barbara G. Walker

http://ffnp.blogspot.com/2013/02/what-could-they-possibly-see-in-each.html

Interspecies Internet – TED talk
http://www.ted.com/talks/the_interspecies_internet_an_idea_in_progress.html

Further Viewing

Alien Nation	*Alien(s)*
Babylon 5	*Constantine*
Deep Space 9	*District 9*
Earth Girls are Easy	*Enemy Mine*
E.T.	*Galaxy Quest*
Highway to Heaven	*Howard the Duck*
King Kong	*Man Who Fell to Earth, The*
Men in Black	*Michael*
Planet of the Apes	*Splash*
Stargate	*Starman*
V	*X-Files*

CHAPTER TEN

TRANSFORMATIVE CHIVALRIC LOVE

A true lover would rather be deprived
of all his money and of everything that
the human mind can imagine as
indispensable to life rather than be without
love, either hoped for or obtained.

The Art of Courtly Love
Andreas Cappellanus

Aspiring to something one cannot have often results in great works of art and humanitarianism. The chosen beloved cannot be had, but that yearning can become fuel for creativity. It's the Muse factor. Yes, sometimes the lovers do actually have sex, but often the "pure love" is more powerful than if the energy were drained away in a regular relationship.

This type of love is slaying dragons and saving virgins. It is about being all that you can be, and more.

Its steps include yearning, surrender, and redemption – all with passionate, pure, unconditional love.

It is tempting but dangerous to look upon the shining face of deity. A safer way is to love a person through whom you can become more spiritual. We seek divinity within each other.

This type of love has as its goal the transformation of the lovers. It's not that one of them sets out to change the other, that's manipulative. In this case though, they become better than they were, because of their aspirational desire to become worthy of the beloved.

The object of Transformative Chivalric Love need not still be alive, as evidenced by the cadres of devotees to various goddesses and icons.

The Defining Myth
Aphrodite/Venus – the Greco-Roman goddess of higher love, true beauty, and passionate romance. As opposed to her son Eros/Cupid, the childish, fun, saucy god of sex and light romance.

Aphrodite embodied the ideals of femininity beauty and passion. This laughter-loving goddess was irresistible and inspired lovers of all sorts...gods, demi-gods, and mortals. Her own liaisons ranged from war god Ares/Mars to Hephaestus/Vulcan, the lame god of the forge.

Living up to the standards of the goddess Aphrodite required strength, passion, and the effort to better yourself in order to be worthy of her.

Exemplar Movie
Shakespeare in Love

Why it exists (evolutionary back-story)
Now we need to get into some metaphysics. If you look at the evolution of life on this planet you see that it all started from single cells and developed complexity and the ability to adapt, right up to today's most amazing artists, statesmen, humanitarians, and scientists. Yet the tube worm did not go extinct just because a mutation occurred and some of them eventually became humans (basically tubeworms with fancy accessories). A logical progression can be observed in biology and in fossil records.

Likewise there is a progression in consciousness. Unless it's sci-fi or fantasy we don't find minerals to be sentient [as long as you don't count computers and A.I., manipulated by humans into a semblance of consciousness]. Plants have sentience – they respond to stimuli in the environment. Someone once said they took the plants-have-feelings so much to heart that they snuck up on their potatoes and knocked them out before baking them. The trees in *The Lord of the Rings* are quite self-conscious. Animals have varying degrees of sentience, then above that consciousness, and in some of the higher species, apparent self-consciousness.

Humans seem to be a leap ahead of animals in self-awareness, though watching the news, reality shows, or photo of Walmartians for a few hours can call that into question. Esoteric schools see humans as the guardians for the advancement of animal souls. Anybody who has pets or works with animals, knows what science is now proving – they have unique personalities and can feel a wide range of emotions.

In any stepped progression you always look for the next step up. According to Mystery School teachings that would be the Kingdom of Conscious Souls – humans who are aware of being souls inhabiting a personality and a body which is the instrument of that soul. A few decades ago the "Indigo Children" were supposed to be harbingers of this evolutionary step. Now most of them live in mom's basement playing computer games all night and day. Not sure if that's upward evolution or not.

According to these philosophies humanity is supposed to be evolving into something greater. Aspirational Love is a tool for that purpose.

How it works (physiology & psychology)

The Mystery Schools propose that human consciousness evolves through three levels: 1) tribal, 2) individual, and 3) group. Non-thinking reactionaries bound to restrictive codes and bent on destroying or being isolated from any others are examples of 1) and you can see them in many of the conflicts around the globe today.

America, like Periclean Greece, Minoan Crete, and other advanced cultures where individuals had rights are given as examples of 2). The downside of American individualism is lack of community, caring, and service to others in the interest of the self. Today's 1% / 99% split and the various rebellions around the planet, from the former Occupy Movement to the Arab Spring, from Syria and Turkey to Brazil and Myanmar, are vivid examples of the difficulty of shifting from 2) to 3).

Level 3) is the ideal put forth in many utopian stories. It's a key factor in what many wanted to see after that supposed 2012 turning point. It is about community, collaboration, and a benign interdependence. Chivalric Love inspires and trains people for this level as well as affording them a fantastic romantic experience.

In Maslow's pyramid illustrating the Hierarchy of Human Needs, the lowest level is food and shelter, the highest level is self- actualization. Chivalric Aspirational Love is meant to raise one to this higher level, where hope lies.

How it serves us now

Goodness knows we can all use some upward aspiration and accomplishment. For too long, humans have been wallowing in our dark ways. Look however at the amazing progress in human rights that has been made in the last hundred years or so. Not everywhere, granted, but in many cultures and countries. The resisters, the holders-on to the backward past, are daily more isolated and are literally fighting for their very existence.

The Muse is an archetype of desire and creativity, as all you writers no doubt know.

We tend to fall in love with an idealization of the other person. Being able to maintain the idealism is essential to maintaining the romance. Sure, you can settle into an ordinary relationship and that can be fine. But the passion, the yearning, the joy of connection at the higher levels is all about art, creativity, and higher energies.

In a world where too many people are too casual about too many things it is difficult to find much idealism. We definitely need more stories around this concept of Aspirational Chivalric Love.

Examples in Myth and Legend
Camelot and the Knights of the Round Table. The love triangle of King Arthur, Guinevere, and Lancelot. Unfortunately, Lancelot and Guinevere did not uphold the laws of chivalry. They dropped from Aspirational Solar Plexus to the Sacral chakra. They should not have had sex, but because they did, the whole kingdom fell apart. It's a great example of what happens when Chivalric Love fails to live up to its own demands.

Marion Zimmer Bradley's *Mists of Avalon* book explores the love life of others caught in this web of chivalric love. Sometimes it works – if they do not have sex. But the failures are tragic and far-reaching.

It's not like the gods mating, it is the higher aspects of humanity falling into the lower. There's nothing wrong with being at that lower sexual level, but it is not the place where you can achieve inspirational Chivalric love.

Vestal Virgins were often not virgins in our modern sense of the term. But the old-fashioned definition meant "ready to receive life". For instance, in pre-Christian systems, after the Mother/Matter/Earth has given birth to the Light/Christ/Sun on the Winter Solstice it is six weeks before she is ready to be impregnated again. At that point, she has once again become "virginal" and the cycle can begin again.

The Christian Virgin Mary and the Egyptian mother goddess Isis both inspire heroic devotion and chivalric actions

The Norse Myth of the Valkyrie Brunhilde and quasi-mortal Siegfried tells of Chivalric Love that unfortunately turns really dark. The setup is that Brunhilde is being punished for disobeying her father, the god Wodin. He puts her to sleep on a rock but she begs him to surround it with a ring of fire so that only the most brave of knights can get to her. Seemingly a good idea. Siegfried breaks through the ring of fire, kisses her, and she awakens to the valiant knight. They swear eternal love but betrayal ensues when he is entrapped by a greedy woman and her brother. It all comes to tears – and flames -- in the end. Another case of Chivalric Love gone south.

Examples in History and Current Events
The Troubadour movement in Provencal France around the 11th century was supported by royalty, especially Eleanor of Aquitaine, who commissioned much of the poetry, art, and music. Chivalry flourished as knights were encouraged to improve and prove themselves for the love of a lady they could never possess, often a queen or the Virgin Mary.

People who go into battle in service to family, a beloved, a regent.

Napoleon and Josephine.

In a case of reverse transformative love you have King Edward VIII of England who abdicated the throne in 1936 to be with his lover, the American divorcee Wallis Simpson, scandalizing the royal family and the country. The movie *The King's Speech* tells how George VI, his younger brother, struggles to fill his place on the throne.

Kids with crushes who try to impress their chosen one. Sometimes it's a teacher, like in the 1950s TV series *Leave it to Beaver.* Also see *Summer of '42* and *My Life as a Dog.*

All artists with Muses. [Refer to "Love of Art", Chapter 6 in this book.]

Examples in Media

Xanadu – it's so bad it's good fun. Olivia Newton John is one of the nine Muses come to life off a Venice California boardwalk mural. Gene Kelly dances, Olivia sings, and everybody roller-skates. Really...?

In *The Lord of the Rings* Eowyn of Rohan holds an admiring aspirational love for Aragorn, the true King. Trying to prove herself worthy of his love, as well as saving the kingdoms, she braves mortal danger on the battlefield and kills the Witch-King...all for a love which she never does obtain.

Joan of Arc.

In *The Fifth Element*, Leeloo is the perfect woman and Korben Dallas [Bruce Willis] tries to become worthy of her. But she informs him she's there to protect him...what's a guy to do? Clean up his act and become the man she needs. It is a fun film with lots of mythic elements in play.

Queen Elizabeth I leads her knights into battle in the film *Elizabeth: The Golden Years.* There's a very inspiring scene as she rides out in shining armor on a white horse to address her troops. You see that every man there has Chivalric adoration for the Queen.

In Dan Brown's *The Da Vinci Code* everyone seems to respect and admire Sophie Neveu, yet no one has sex with her. Others are there to serve her and it is not until the end of the story that her elevated sense of destiny is revealed to be real...she is a direct descendant of Jesus and Mary Magdalene. The Priory de Zion swears fealty to her in an example of Aspirational Chivalric Love.

Braveheart, Ladyhawk, and *The Four Feathers* offer relationships of Chivalric Love.

The TV series *Spartacus* Season 1, Episode 7 begins with the words, "...the man you could become", a prefect Chivalric Love line.

Examples in Music
"Love Lifts Us Up Where We Belong" by Joe Cocker.
"I'll Make a Man out of You" – *Mulan* film
In "Long Black Veil" the man was doing the wrong thing -- having an affair with his best friend's wife -- until he did the right thing by taking the rap for a crime he did not commit rather than expose her.
Troubadour songs of Provence
"On the street where you live."

Symbols
Hearts
Pedestals
Uplifted hands, arms, eyes
Reaching for something just out of reach
Stars, constellations
Bright, almost blinding light as one gazes at the beloved
A halo

Key Element – The Shining Moment
Stepping up into the higher mode. If you can actually make it a physical stepping-up, all the better.

Putting aside the old ways, things, or actions. E.g., someone always carried a gun, then they put it down.

Written Descriptions

Use inspiring words: aspiration, uplifting, elevating, inspiring, energizing.

Show us the transition of the person being transformed by making a clear delineation between how they are before the change and how they are after it.

Let us see that the transformed person experiences the environment differently before and after they fall in love and achieve a higher state of mind. E.g. grumbling about the heat and tourists and smog on Hollywood Boulevard versus finding Marilyn Monroe's star, kneeling down and placing flowers upon it.

Switch from clumsy, unthinking handling of an object dear to the love object to careful, protective handling.

Cinematic Techniques

The upward shot from the one being inspired up-angle to the object of affection, the Muse.

The reverse down-angle.

The larger (typically) males getting on their knees to swear allegiance, subjugating themselves and looking up to the object of adoration.

Put something behind the object that symbolizes that higher ideal, e.g. a cross, a flag, the icon at the center of the search, etc.

Raising the light level. And typically also using smoke so the light is diffused to give a more ethereal look.

Conclusion

You want your character who yearns with Chivalric Love to ultimately be transformed and to say or live some version of the quote, "I have decided to become the person you think I am".

In a world steeped in armed conflict, crude comedy, reality shows, shallow if any values, we really need more stories featuring Chivalric Aspirational Love to uplift our hearts and minds.

The power of story is amazing and as story-tellers you can help raise our vision and our actions as we learn from and are inspired by your characters.

As the saying goes – "Onward and Upward!"

*****

Exercise #1 – Awareness

What is an example of love noticeably and lastingly changing someone for the better - in myth, history, media, current reality.

*****

Exercise #2 – Writing

Write a scene where the character deals with another in a regular non-aspirational, individually or tribally based consciousness.

Write the same scene with the character coming from the higher aspirational, chivalric consciousness.

****

Further Reading

Arthurian Romances - Chrétien de Troyes
Chivalry: The Path of Love – Chronicle Books
Dreams of Love and Fateful Encounters – Dr. Ethel Person
Idylls of the King – Alfred, Lord Tennyson
Inner Drives – Pamela Jaye Smith
Life Against Death – Norman O. Brown

Mists of Avalon – Marian Zimmer Bradley
Plague of Provence – Nina Ansley
Power of the Dark Side, The – Pamela Jaye Smith
Symbols.Images.Codes – Pamela Jaye Smith
White Goddess, The – Robert Graves

Further Viewing
Almost Famous
As Good as it Gets
Camelot
Dave
Excalibur
It's a Wonderful Life
Lord of the Rings – series of films
Love, Actually
Milk Money
Moulin Rouge
Parsival – opera by Richard Wagner
Princess Bride, The
Spartacus

CHAPTER ELEVEN

BREAKING UP IS HARD TO DO

"Heav'n hath no rage like love to hatred turn'd,
Nor Hell a fury, like a woman scorn'd."

William Congreve (1670-1729)

At the end of the 20th century the most-played, most-purchased, most-requested song was the 1964 Righteous Brothers' romantic lament -- "You've lost that lovin' feeling". Its popularity is evidence that most people have broken up with someone, or had someone break up with them.

Boy finds girl, boy loses girl, boy gets girl back. Okay, that's the rom-com formula. But the more dramatic and psychologically interesting stories come when love is lost, for whatever reason, and heartbreak ensues. Then through valiant and heroic efforts love is won back against all odds. Or not.

The separation of the lovers or potential lovers is essential to the drama. In your stories breaking up should be very hard to do for at least one of the characters and should have difficult reverberations for both of them and often others around them.

This category is about one person making a personal decision and taking personal action to break up with the other person. It does not include unwanted separation as from war, disaster, or death. If both people decide to break up and there're no hard feelings, it's not in this category because that is easy to do, not hard to do.

The Defining Myth
When Greek hero Jason and his pals the Argonauts went to get the Golden Fleece, Jason brought back the local princess and sorceress Medea as his bride. They were hot for each other and all went well for a number of years, including the birth of two sons. Then politics intervened and ambitious Jason was easily talked into marrying a local princess since the people didn't really like that "foreign witch" Medea. Jason announced the impending marriage and told her he'd have to put her aside. Medea said she understood politics and would even throw an engagement party for the new bride. She did, but she also killed the girl at the party with an acid-laced dress. To further hurt the faithless Jason and complete the devastation of her heart, she even killed their two little boys and then fled the land in a chariot pulled by dragons.

Exemplar Movie
My Best Friend's Wedding [humourous] & *Fatal Attraction* [deadly]

Why it exists (evolutionary back-story)
Making bonds, breaking up, making new bonds...it might be to keep the gene-pool stirred up as more genetic diversity generally equals more healthy people. Biology gears us towards non-monogamy (especially in males), most likely in the service of increasing good traits and dropping off weak ones.

In a recent study about adultery in America, 60% of married men and 40% of married women admitted to extra-marital sex. And that's only the number of people who answered honestly. How many of those affairs then resulted in break-ups?

Lifetime monogamy is a romantic construct and an expression of refined emotions, but is not a biological instinct. Rare are the number of animals that mate for life. *Scientific American* magazine lists some swans, mice, rodents, and a few other species . From the rampant sexual profligacy of our cousins the bonobos to the notoriously promiscuous cuckoo birds (after whom the word cuckold came) even if two animals mate, they do not stay sexually faithful. Depending on the species, from 10-30% of the young in mated relationships are the offspring of another.

Human males seem to have developed in ways to ensure their sperm fertilizes the female's egg. Each ejaculation contains three types of sperm: the path-finders, the killers, and the survivors. The path-finders clear a way through for the swimmers. The killers destroy the sperm of any other male. The survivors swim through to the egg and one of them may fertilize it. The evolutionary situation to develop this trait is the presumption that the sperm of competing males will be present simultaneously in the female.

Another competition device is the fierce sexual activity after a fight, breakup, or separation – that famous "makeup sex". The robust thrusting and the shape of the penis creates a suction pump that fairly effectively vacuums away any competing sperm. Again, the evolutionary impetus is the presumption of invader sperm from some other male, most often with the acquiescence or at the invitation of the female.

How it works (physiology & psychology)
Falling in love has been likened to a chemical addiction. The release of dopamines, serotonin, and the bonding chemical oxytocin is a real rush. Whoever co-creates that with you becomes the supplier of good feelings. It's not difficult to get addicted to the lover's voice, touch, presence...and to those orgasms. The lover is a delivery mechanism for ecstasy and easily becomes a "drug of choice".

Depending on how dependent one is on those chemicals, a break-up can throw the switch into withdrawal mode. Just as getting off any other chemical addiction causes very real and quite uncomfortable physical symptoms and psychological imbalances, so too can a romantic breakup.

Contrary to the book *He's Just Not That Into You*, sometimes a guy will withdraw because he is very much into you and that scares the life out of him. Those excellent highs, the seductive ecstasy...there's a real chance you'll get so absorbed into the other person that you'll lose yourself. Commitment issues may often be related to sheer self-preservation, even if not consciously realized. Keep in mind the Judeo-Christian wedding liturgy where a man takes a wife and they "become one". Pretty scary if you are still trying to figure out who you are, are an adventurous person, or just treasure your independence. Some people break up to avoid those issues, as in *Runaway Bride.*

Another psychological trope is people so uncomfortable about being the "bad guy/girl" that they stay with someone they do not love anymore.

Those who are terrified of breaking up with an abusive partner is a really dark side of this concept, as in *Sleeping With the Enemy* and *The Burning Bed.*

Jealousy and revenge are often seen as social control mechanisms to keep order in a group. Any society dependent on the transfer of wealth through genetic lines and the wielding of power through male lines will by definition need to ensure the purity of bloodlines. Adultery and promiscuity are direct threats to the social norms and are punished. Stoning is still popular in some cultures, and in Texas a man is still considered within his rights to shoot another man having sex with his wife, as long as it's in his own bed. It's considered trespassing and a threat to his property. These situations often lead to break-ups, particularly among more conservative people.

How it serves us now

Some pairings are about relationship, home, security. That's all fine and good. The more intense and interesting ones are passionate romances that are about deeper issues: archetypes, life themes such as abandonment or loyalty, personal awareness, growth to one's higher possibilities. Or in tragedies, a fall into the abyss of one's own shadow.

People who keep breaking up and then forming new relationships with a version of the same person have not yet resolved some inner personality issues. Once that is realized and dealt with they can move on to healthier, longer-lasting relationships. Watching a character keep making the same mistakes can be funny or tragic or poignant.

The push-pull polarity of breaking up then making up may be the only adrenalin rush and oxytocin infusion some people get, particularly if they are stuck in boring jobs [or these days, no jobs at all], have tiresome relatives, shallow friends, and no uplifting outside interests. It's the concept of "I'd rather feel *something*, even pain, than to feel nothing at all".

"It's not you, it's me...honestly." Well, that's a recipe for conflict. Who is it really? You can get good mileage out of this one as you reveal what or who really is at fault in the break-up.

And never forget William Congreve's observation in *The Mourning Bride*, "Heaven has no rage like love to hatred turned, Nor hell a fury like a woman scorned". The downside of breaking up can be abuse, stalking, and sometimes death – too often the death of innocent parties such as children.

Too often the person whose love has waned does not want to be the "bad guy" so they stay in a relationship that is quickly deflating. Both parties are burdened by the relationship that used to buoy them up. One is desperately hanging on and hoping that love will return. The other is trying to be kind but is actually keeping them from moving on and finding someone else who really does love them. If you have this situation in your story, the turning point for change could be the character hearing and acting on adages such as, "The quickest cut is the kindest", "Sometimes you have to be cruel to be kind", "Do not torture before you kill".

Some people are so reluctant to break up they try to drive the other person away by treating them like dirt, to make them be the one who initiates the breakup so that they can feel better about themselves.

And also, sometimes to leave the other person with a feeling of dignity and control they would not otherwise have had.

Examples in Myth and Legend
In Homer's *Iliad* Menelaus's queen Helen ran off with Paris, prince of Troy. Menelaus refused to accept the breakup and gathered up all the warriors in Greece, sailed to Troy in a thousand ships, and laid siege to the city for ten years. All to get his wife back.

After the fall of Troy, Prince Aeneas was destined to go found Rome so he set out from the smoking ruins bound for the other side of Italy. On a long stop-over at Carthage he got romantically entangled with their Queen Dido. She totally adored him and welcomed him into her arms, her bed, and her throne room. The god Mercury eventually had to remind Aeneas of his mission. Aeneas and his men bid farewell to their local loves and set sail. Heart-broken, Queen Dido built a huge funeral pyre atop a cliff and threw herself upon it. Once again Aeneas left something he loved in smoking ruins as he sailed off to a new adventure.

Southwest native Americans have the myth of La Llorona, a woman scorned who drowned her children in a river and whose mourning voice can be heard in the waters.

From the Bible comes a breakup whose bad blood still troubles the world. The patriarch Abraham's wife Sarah was barren. He needed a son so he took their maid Hagar to wife and she bore him Ishmael. Then Sarah miraculously became pregnant with Isaac and made Abraham get ride of Hagar and Ishmael. The Jews are said to be of the line of Isaac and the Arabs from the line of Ishmael.

Examples in History and Current Events
England's King Henry VIII was notorious for breaking up with his wives...usually in deadly ways.

In 1994, South Carolina woman Susan Smith could not break up with her husband, and her lover threatened her with a breakup because he didn't want kids. So she drowned her two little boys and claimed they had been kidnapped. This replay of the Medea myth happens way too often with mothers and sometimes fathers, taking their despair and hatred out on the children.

NASA astronaut Lisa Nowak sped cross-country in flight-suit diapers to confront her rival. Obviously not a well-managed break-up.

Ask your friends and no doubt search your own life for examples of good or bad break-ups. How many have managed to stay friends with their exes? Or for some is it like the George Strait song, "All my exes live in Texas, that's why I live in Tennessee"?

Examples in Media
"Men cheat, women cry, people die – it's opera." So says the poster. Bizet's opera *Carmen* is a great example of a series of breakups that go really bad.

In *Top Gun*, Maverick (Tom Cruise) sings 'You've lost that lovin' feeling" to Charlie (Kelly McGillis) the first time they meet at a bar.

(500) Days of Summer

Famous breakup quotes include "Frankly, my dear, I don't give a damn", Rhett Butler to Scarlet O'Hara in *Gone with the Wind* on the 'love her but can't put up with her' side. "We'll always have Paris", Rick to Ilsa in *Casablanca* in the 'love her and want her but a greater duty calls' side.

How to Lose a Guy in Ten Days – this rom-com is a series of intentional breakups that don't take.

In *The Night Porter* it's so difficult for Charlotte Rampling's character to break away from the Nazi (Dirk Bogarde) who tortured her during the War, that she comes back to him afterwards to continue their dark relationship.

Madame Butterfly and *Anna Karenina* are versions of the Dido & Aeneas myth as both women kill themselves over a breakup and the loss of passionate love.

Fatal Attraction is an example of a really bad break-up that ends with a boiled bunny, attempted murder, and an accidental death.

My Best Friend's Wedding is a bittersweet break-up. *Runaway Bride* is about a commitment-phobic woman who keeps breaking up at the altar.

The Crying Game is a story of reluctant love, uncomfortable discovery, breaking up, then coming back together.

Bed and Sofa, a 1925 Russian silent movie, is the story of two brothers and the wife of one of them. The married brother doesn't have a job, the other brother does. He comes to stay and soon couples up with the wife. The husband is moved out to the sofa and the brother moves into bed with the wife. The rest of the story is about the husband attempting to overcome the break up and get off the sofa and back into the marriage bed.

Both *The Break Up Artist* [from a guy's POV] and *The Break-Up Artist* [from a girl's POV].

Examples in Music
So many songs are about breaking up and the loss of love; here are just a few.
"How can you heal a broken heart?" – Al Green ["We were never told about the sorrow."]
"Breaking up is hard to do" – Neal Sedaka
"The Thrill is Gone" – B.B. King
Country-Western songs – pick just about any one of them.
"I fall to pieces" – Patsy Cline
"I've got your picture, she's got you" - Patsy Cline
"Piece of my Heart" – Janis Joplin
"The First Cut is the Deepest" – Cat Stevens
"Who's Making Love to Your Fool, Lady, While You're Out Making Love?" - Blues Brothers
"Why You Drinking Like the Night Is Young" – Holly Williams
"Yesterday" – The Beatles
"You were Always on my Mind" – Willie Nelson
http://en.wikipedia.org/wiki/You've_Lost_That_Lovin'_Feelin'

Symbols
Cracks
Shattered glass
Frayed rope ends
Separate tables
Stretched to the breaking point
Boiled rabbit

Key Element – The Shining Action

That commitment to leaving -- walking away, shutting the door, closing the diary, tearing up the letter, bursting into tears, etc. Show us the impact moment of the break-up and how both parties handle it -- that is where your drama lies.

It's Rhett Butler walking away from Scarlett O'Hara in *Gone with the Wind*.

It is not Rick sitting at the table getting drunk in *Casablanca*. It's the good-bye at the airport with him accepting fate and convincing Ilsa that she needs to go with Lazlo and stay with the cause.

On the other side of the breaking up equation, there is Madame Butterfly committing hari kari and Anna Karenina throwing herself under a train.

Written Descriptions

Set up the breakup by foreshadowing the trait, the threat, the character weakness, the outside influence, etc. that will eventually be the trigger for one lover to break up with the other. It's often noted that all those little eccentricities you find so adorable at the beginning of a relationship are what will drive you crazy three years in. Give us at least one of those as a pivot point for the final decision.

This subject lends itself to the non-linear approach. The breakup itself can occur at any time, depending on the type of story you are telling. Does your story start with a breakup and then it's about getting back together? Is the story about leading up to the break-up and the break-up is in the final act? Or does the break-up occur earlier on but the story continues after that? Is the breakup the climax or just a stepping stone?

Determining the emphasis of the breakup will determine how much time you spend on it, how much detail you get into with setting the scene, internal dialogue, character action, symbolism, etc. How many pages of prose or script does the breakup need to find its proper place in your story? Answering the questions in the previous paragraph can help you determine the appropriate emphasis for the actual breakup.

Show us what happens after the break-up. Do the two people just go their own ways? Do they shift the relationship and become "just friends"? Does the dumpee become a stalker? Does the dumper have second thoughts and try to get back with the other person? And how does that work? Do people die?

They do not use the little pet names anymore. It's not, "Hi, punkin' doodle"; now it's "Hello", or "Oh...you." The gestures of affection are either non-existent or aborted, e.g. through force of habit she starts to ruffle his hair, then pulls back.

From "I" hugs to "A" hugs. They go from hugs where the entire bodies stand close together forming the letter "I" to hugs where they stand apart and lean in with only the arms and heads touching, forming an "A" shape.

Use words such as split, shatter, break, decompose and such to describe other things; they'll lend a resonance to the emotional situation. E.g. tree limbs cracking off and falling in the storm, the crackle of ice on the frozen pond, the cookie crumbles, someone rips a ring-tab off a can, the moldy left-overs in the back of the fridge, someone's old coffee cup that no one else uses, the car that won't start.

Cinematic Techniques
The relationship between up and down angles reveals a dynamic. The person getting screwed is always looking up. The dumper has the power and that is shown by their downward angle towards the dumpee.

If the story evolves and there is a change in the dynamic between the people such as the dumpee somehow rekindling the fire or becoming a friend, that change is shown by the change of the camera angle between them – it's now more on an equal level since the perceived power is now more equal.

During the giddy days of being in love, the camera could circle around them, implying the dizzy spin of emotions. When love dies, the camera becomes more static, particularly for the person who has lost that loving feeling.

Changing the lighting from bright to darker, changing the colour scheme from goldens to blues...are symbolic of the shifting emotions in your characters.

Conclusion
You've got a rich character choice between telling this story from the point of view of the breaker and/or the breakee. Each one's experience of the break-up is probably worlds apart and rife with strong emotions.

Sex can be revived but you can't revive love. Trying to do so can however make for very interesting drama and hot story points. It can also complicate things for a new relationship as the lingering physical attraction with the old flame gets in the way of the new one.

The dynamics of breaking up offer you worlds of nuanced situations in which to build character arcs and story arcs. Giving us some of the mythology, psychology, and biology of how it all works can add interesting complexity to your stories without detracting from the main event – the love relationship or the impending lack thereof.

*****

Exercise #1 – Awareness
What is the most dramatic break-up you have seen in books, media, or real life?

*****
Exercise #2 – Writing
Write a break-up scene where your character is no longer in love and is breaking up with someone they still like, but just don't have the passion for anymore. They don't want to hurt the other person, but can no longer be in the romantic relationship the other person still desires. [And do not use the "let's just be friends" line.]

Write a break-up scene where your character is still madly, passionately in love with someone but they are driven to break up with them. Reasons might be they have done something horrible to your character (or mistakenly think they have), for the sake of the children, to restore integrity and self-respect, to save the free world as in *Casablanca*, to save the kingdom, to save the cosmos.

*****
Further Reading
Anna Karenina
Dreams of Love and Fateful Encounters – Dr. Ethel Person
Great Expectations – Charles Dickens [the Miss Haversham character]
He's Just Not That Into You - Greg Behrendt and Liz Tuccillo
Inner Drives: Create Characters Using the Chakras – Pamela Jaye Smith
Life Against Death – Norman O. Brown
Madame Bovary
Power of the Dark Side – Pamela Jaye Smith
Symbols.Images.Codes – Pamela Jaye Smith

Further Viewing
9-1/2 Weeks	*Anna Karenina*
Cleopatra	*Dangerous Liaisons*
Gone With the Wind	*Heart Like a Wheel*
Lord of the Rings – Aragorn breaking up with Eowyn of Rohan	
My Super Ex Girlfriend	*Play Misty for Me*
Rome – the HBO series	*Sessions*
Sleeping with the Enemy	*Tudors, The*
Unfaithful	

CHAPTER TWELVE

LOVE OF COMMUNITY
Civil Society

Organization is indispensable; for liberty arises and has meaning only within a self-regulating community of free co-operating individuals. But, though indispensable, organization can also be fatal. Too much organization transforms men and women into automata, suffocates the creative spirit and abolishes the very possibility of freedom. As usual, the only safe course is in the middle, between the extremes of *laissez-faire* at one end of the scale and of total control at the other.

Brave New World Revisited – Aldous Huxley

"This nation, this generation, in this hour has man's first chance to build a Great Society, a place where the meaning of man's life matches the marvels of man's labor."

President Lyndon B. Johnson, announcing his new domestic programs in 1964

*****

Civil society is a self-imposed structure held together by those individuals dedicated to its vision, which is to improve the living conditions and quality of life of the community. People's love of their community can find outlet and value in the organizations of civil society. Not everybody has to belong to the organizations but everybody can benefit from them, be they the Lions Club, the Junior League, the local YMCA and VFW [Veterans of Foreign Wars], religious organizations, and the like.

Today's accepted definition of civil society is organizations that are non-governmental, but for the purposes of effective story-telling we are defining civil society as above family and below the nation or the state. Though it does include local government (the dogcatcher to the mayor) it does not include larger governments (state and federal), the military, and larger businesses. The mom-and-pop hardware store on Main Street is part of the civil society. The big box store at the edge of town is not. The interconnectedness that creates and sustains civil society is about looking in at your immediate community, more than looking out at the broader world, or down at the bottom line. It's local.

In this chapter, responsibility to and love for your community helps to establish and support local participatory democracies, be they in government, social organizations, etc. Writer and political commentator Michael Ventura says it well, "... (That) brings to the surface the most basic question: What is my responsibility (*to my society*)? In a democracy, that is the basic question for any citizen."

In effective stories centered around the love of community there is a very real danger that can tear apart or destroy the fabric of that civil society. In *High Noon* the town gives up its responsibility to support the sheriff, who is defending their town from iconic bad guy Frank Miller. The same thing happens with the League of Shadows in Batman's Gotham. In the comedy *In and Out*, prejudice against gays threatens the otherwise close-knit and generally accepting community.

In these stories, the quality of life in the community can often entail your protagonists fighting against profit-driven corporations and special interest groups such as big oil, big agriculture, big pharma, the weapons industry, etc.

On the positive side for your characters, civil society provides the medium for the growth of and promotes the development of local arts, sciences, etc. Everyone in the community, young and old alike, can enjoy and benefit from scout groups and 4H, science fairs, art shows on the courthouse lawn, holiday festivals and parades.

Civil society is "We the People" in action.

The Defining Myth
Camelot, the Shining City on the Hill.

Exemplar Movie
It's a Wonderful Life

Why it exists (evolutionary back-story)
The first human societies were nomadic, following migrating herds. Hunting larger animals required a division of labor: runners to hunt it down and kill it, people to butcher it, dress it and carry it back to camp, women to cook and serve it (and clean up afterwards), and story-tellers to entertain the tribe around the campfire.

When food is cooked, its nutritional content goes up. Man began to climb up out of the primordial stew when he started to cook. It's one step and tens of thousands of years from that first primitive grill to a Texas barbecue joint.

Once humans figured out how to plant crops, preserve and store food, and domesticate animals they were able to settle down in one place. Moving from the hunter-gatherer mode to the more agrarian mode helped to foster the growth of art, religion, commerce, and government.

Stories about communal activities were among the very first stories ever told; early cave art shows humans hunting in groups. The art was typically in places where groups of humans gathered to hear stories, and the flickering fires created the first animation art. See Werner Herzog's illustrative documentary *Cave of Forgotten Dreams*.

How it works (physiology & psychology)

The human species is by nature gregarious, though there are always hermits, misanthropes, sociopaths, and downright psychopaths, but for the most part people like to congregate and share their experiences of living and loving, suffering and hope. They want to be witnesses of each others' lives. As the African proverb goes, "It takes a village".

Life can be hard. In some societies life can be really, really hard. As 17th century British philosopher Thomas Hobbes observed, "Life is solitary, poor, nasty, brutish, and short". The comfort of the group goes a long way to alleviating the pain of death and suffering, particularly tragic early deaths or the ravages of disease.

Recent scientific discoveries show that levels of testosterone dropped with the development of technology. That makes sense when you see tools, agriculture, and animal husbandry all as force-multipliers to increase resources and lower labor costs and danger...thus the lowered demand for heavy testosterone.

Though it does not apply to loners, love of acceptance by the group is a powerful driver for most people, as exemplified in clubs, cliques, tribes, and gangs.

It's a short step from tribal taboos and customs (against incest, for body marking) to societal or religious commandments (honor the parents so when you are one, you yourself get honored in turn), and then to more formal legal systems such as the Code of Hammurabi in 18th century BCE Babylon. These guidelines are about personal behaviour, yet they apply to the entire community. When everyone takes personal responsibility and follows them, you ideally have a supportive and peaceful civil society.

Besides the obvious benefits of resource acquisition and allocation, a good civil society also improves people's health and well-being. Professor Francesco Billari, from University of Oxford Department of Sociology said: "People who trust others seem to report better health and greater happiness. The study of social trust therefore has wider implications in public health, governmental policy and private charity, and there are good reasons to think that governments, religious groups and other civic organizations should try to cultivate more trust in society. Social trust has become an increasingly important topic for academics, who want to understand the causes of better health and greater happiness within society." [Science Daily March 2014]

Gossips are often scorned but they do serve a purpose for the group. People who cheat the local system threaten the resources of others and the gossips are like the canaries in coal mines, the lookouts in a prairie dog town, or a tornado siren -- they warn of danger.

Manners are rules of behaviour specific to cultures, times, and places. What is considered polite in one society may be considered offensive in another. Manners also change radically over time. At one time, opening a door for a lady marked a man as a gentleman; now it marks him as hopelessly old-fashioned or even patronizing. A challenge for traders and travelers has always been how to navigate the manners of different cultures, and applies even more so today. Manners can be indicators of the class structure of a community. From the foppish manners of European courtly life to the precise protocols of the Chinese Empires, one's grasp of the intricacies were like a secret language that the other classes did not know. American novelists Henry James and Edith Wharton used manners to illustrate the class level of various characters and create conflict as those levels clashed, such as in James's *The Wings of the Dove* and Wharton's *The House of Mirth*.

In times when man does not totally control his environment he has to rely on other people. The way you make that happen is by having the social lubricant of good manners, being gracious and hospitable – like Australian bloke *Crocodile Dundee* in New York City.

In today's ever-changing digital world, who knows what manners really are... and fewer people than ever have them.

Isolationism does not support survival. Out on the vast Great Plains of the American Midwest, most people wave greetings when meeting each other on the often empty highways, even if it's just a raised finger (no, not that one; that's for the freeways). A person never knows when they'll break down out on that lonely road and need someone's help. Unfortunately, this practice seems to have gone away in many parts of America and the world.

Mythic Meaning
Myths are the stories we tell ourselves to explain the world around us and within us; and to teach us how to best engage with those worlds.

The idea of paradise seems to be inherent in human nature. We know that some animals have a sense of fairness, so part of our yearning for the idyllic community may be based on evolutionary drives for resource acquisition and allocation.

Then for most of us there is a sense that we issued forth from a perfect (pre-natal) environment that totally supported us into a world where we were increasingly separated from the mother and became more isolated in our individual self, sometimes not to our advantage. It's easy to see how the yearning for bygone days of total well-being gets translated into paradise and perfect societies.

Given the very rich human imagination it is also easy to see how that personal desire gets projected onto the larger canvas of a perfect tribe, culture, world, cosmos and beyond, even to other dimensions. Somewhere there must be that perfection we all dimly yet deeply recall and which if fortunate, good, disciplined, courageous, and/or loving enough we can regain.

As Joseph Campbell pointed out in his series *The Masks of God*, people create religions that reflect their surroundings: pantheism thrives in complex geographies with many varieties of flora and fauna while the major monotheisms have come from barren desert lands.

Some say "As above, so below" and that we are instinctively trying to create here on earth a remembered heaven from whence we came. Others note that as science reveals more about the order of the cosmos, from clusters of galaxies to the smallest sub-atomic particle, we can better understand why the human mind perceives and imposes order: we're all just part of an unfathomably complex yet ultimately ordered universe within which randomness and chaos occur.

Camelot – the ideal place, a 'shining city on a hill' – is a prototype of a perfect civil society where a good king rules the land with the help of noble knights, a fair queen, and a wise wizard advisor. Damsels are protected from evil-doers, dragons are slain, and invaders repelled. The symbol of King Arthur's round table makes all who are present equal participants. Under Arthur's rule, these ideal knights followed the highest aspects of the Warrior Code: to protect and defend the weak and the innocent, and to uphold and promote the good, the true, and the beautiful. Gentility and honour were the gracious by-products of this perfect civil society and *noblesse oblige* prevailed: the fortunate gave of their largesse to the less fortunate.

Unfortunately, human weakness brought about the downfall of Camelot, just as most other paradises were plagued by people's frailties, arrogance, or downright evilness.

Most mythologies include a Golden Age which sets the pattern for the ideal civil society. They also include an explanation of why it failed. We have a strong sense of how things should be, but not a whole lot of success recreating that in real life.

How it serves us now
To make a better life, man has created a compact among his peers. Working together in common sacrifice and shared responsibilities has led to stronger and more civil societies. As long as all members of those groups work in concert, that compact remains strong and vibrant.

Unfortunately in our increasingly interconnected yet socially fractured world, few citizens are actually involved in any local physical civil society and do not share responsibilities for the local quality of life. Many do not know their neighbors' names, shop at big box stores rather than whatever local markets might remain, and in notorious cases don't even come to the aid of someone being dangerously attacked – and sometimes killed – in their own neighborhood.

Yet it would be a mistake to dismiss the digital age as having no value as a device of civil society. Use of the internet has created opportunities for coalitions that have led to the election of Barack Obama, the Arab Spring, the international Occupy Movement, flash mobs, and global support groups for various concerns from wounded warriors to breast cancer, and actions ecological, political and commercial, including strikes and boycotts.

The extended arms of mega corporations have the capacity to dominate commerce and any entrepreneur who would otherwise compete with that corporation. Their concerns are for the stockholders, not for the populace where they are operating.

Civil societies may fracture when the citizenry is no longer committed to the compact that has held them together. But a larger problem is a loss of faith in the ideals (or the mythology) that create a civil society, be it that of the neighborhood or of the town.

Changing demographics (because of people moving in or out of a community, or of money flowing in or out) can play havoc with the systems of a civil society as different ideologies, agendas, and cultural norms come into conflict with each other.

Yet even in the midst of the dissolution of a society, culture, or civilization there are usually small pockets of people dedicated to creating a better way of life. Through their concerted efforts they make anew the compact of a civil society that may include barter systems, local agriculture, going green, B corporations, the rebirth of commitment to the community, possibly the integration of other cultures, and the re-formation of the social compact. When that occurs, people once again bind together into a civil society.

Examples in Myth and Legend
Because the yearning for paradise, for the return of the lost Golden Age, is universal, you find stories about the perfect community in mythologies all around the world.

In addition to Camelot, the British Isles also gave us the lost lands of Avalon and of Lyonesse, sunk beneath the seas to the west. Hawaiians have a similar legend, as do the Hopi and the Aztecs. As we learn more about the rise and fall of sea levels associated with ice ages, some of these lost-land legends turn out to be based on ancient facts, as underwater archaeology is revealing. The running theme in these myths is peacefulness, equality of rights regardless of rank or profession, and prosperity for all.

The myths (or perhaps actual facts passed down in stories) about Atlantis have captivated imaginations for millennia. The Greeks Solon and Plato, Francis Bacon, Ignatious Donnelly, Madame Helena Blavatsky, and Edgar Cayce all wrote about that cultured civilization where everyone worked together and prospered...until things started going bad, sometimes because of humans, sometimes because of nature. Most stories about Atlantis are heavy on the details of its civil society.

In the Bible the Promised Land is called the land of milk and honey. The Australian Aborigines' Dreamtime is paradisiacal as are the origin myths of the African Bantu. The Cheyenne and Iroquois, the natives of Amazonia and other South American peoples all tell of ancient perfect societies.

Other myths and legends include: Chaco Canyon and the Anasazi of the American southwest, in southeast Africa Great Zimbabwe, whose ruins are still not fully understood. Mohenjo-Doro in western India was the first planned city yet discovered. They had sewers and toilets with seats. A legendary city said to be further out in the Indian Ocean was discovered a few years ago, right where the myths said it would be.

Shangri-La (Shamballa) is located somewhere in Tibet, or eastern China, or the Gobi Desert, or the Altai Mountains, or perhaps Nepal. This ancient perfect society whose cities are sometimes said to be made of glass and include escalators, graceful fountains, and technology so advanced that it makes ours look like children's building blocks, has inspired books and movies (*Lost Horizon*), games, and even figured into some Nazi plans for world domination and the imposition of their idea of the perfect civil society.

Explore further in the many books and websites about lost, ancient, mythical places – keeping in mind that they are a projected pattern of our own ideals. Or maybe our ideals are a result of some ancient passed-down or genetic memory of the perfect civil society.

Examples in History and Current Events

<u>THE AMERICAN EXPERIMENT</u>

It wasn't so long ago that most Americans west of the Appalachia Mountains did not have a civil society but rather, the fierce anarchy of the Wild West. The process of progress took much growing, experimenting, and learning brought about by the desire to create and the dedication to make happen a civil society.

Community is always local, but local community can well lead the way towards regionalism and nationalism. Yet there will always be a sense of unity and localism.
What happens in Detroit is not what happens in Houston, LA, New York. And yet people everywhere want the same things: safe, stable, prosperous, thriving communities that work well for everybody.

We will look at three stages in the formation of a civil society, using early America as an example. Moving your story from one stage to another, or using all three stages, will give you opportunities for dramatic shifts. Your characters will be pressured to change; some will lead the change, some will easily follow along, some will refuse to change, and others will take serious action to prevent change. It can all be the stuff of drama.

1. <u>The Rugged Individual</u>

There were many reasons for a rugged individual shying away from society. Sometimes they were motivated by Love of Adventure, sometimes they were on the run from the law or bad situations, and sometimes they were just anti-social.

Trail-blazers were the people who first ventured westward, normally alone in the deserts, the mountains, and the open prairies. In this stage of development they had to be multi-talented and be able to multi-task in order to survive. For lack of the law, many of these people found justice on their own terms when necessary.

There were individuals who could embrace the change from wilderness to the beginnings of civilized communities, and those who could not. One evolved and the other disappeared to become the rogue or the lone wolf.

Examples are Jeremiah Johnson, Kit Carson, Jim Bridger, Jedediah Smith, and Clint Eastwood's character in *The Unforgiven*.

2. The Boomtown Phase

When success overwhelms a town or community, its inability to respond to the increasing demands placed on the infrastructure strains the ties that support civil society.

Newcomers don't necessarily share that sense of responsibility. They're just there to get in, get rich, and get out. Many thriving communities created by the exploitation of precious metals, fur, timber, oil, cattle, etc. turn to ghost towns after the bust that follows every boom.

The Boomtown phase is typically corrupt. The TV series *Deadwood,* set in the late 1800s South Dakota, is an excellent dramatization of this aspect of the process. So is *Hell on Wheels,* about the growing railroad industry around Cheyenne Wyoming.

With the developing oil shale industry, the current day Dakotas are experiencing a modern boom-and-bust cycle due to fluctuations in the price of oil. During the boom phase thousands of people have gone there to work in the oil and gas fields. Lack of housing and schools, lack of roads, lack of enough law enforcement...this lack of infrastructure has predictably resulted in the proliferation of crime, drugs and prostitution reminiscent of the old Deadwood.

The small Texas town of Burkburnette boomed with the discovery of oil in 1912. Within four years the town grew to 20,000 people. The inherent drama of the situation was the basis for the 1940 film *Boom Town* starring Clark Gable and Spencer Tracy.

Other examples of boomtowns are Sutter's Mill California, Dodge City Kansas, Tombstone Arizona, and many more.

The same problems might also arise in space colonization.

3. The Formation of a Civil Society

The growth of civil society in America west of the Mississippi River begins back when ranchers would drive their herds across hundreds of miles of open range to the railheads, where cattle were loaded onto trains and taken to the slaughterhouses, such as in Kansas City and Chicago.

Cow towns grew up around the railroads and the cattle trails. Once barbed wire was introduced and the railroads expanded, long cattle drives were not as necessary. These growing towns then needed sheriffs, doctors, mayors, churches, feed stores, schools and schoolmarms. It was the desire of people to have a peaceful and prosperous existence that led to a more concerted effort to craft workable civil societies.

In any group a few individuals will always have a vision of something greater than what exists; they see that the sum of the parts can be greater than the whole. Those people bring others on board and eventually the group effort leads to a group consciousness where people rise above just their own individual interests. That commitment to the common good then fosters individual responsibility and sacrifice – because ideally, everybody wins.

The organizations created by and for a small community expanded the reach of that community. They offered people the opportunity to come together and to unite in some common cause, be it at dances, churches, fairs, fellowship lodges, quilting bees, a barn-raising, a school, or a pot-luck dinner. All were meant to draw in the cross section of the people of the community and thus made the community stronger as everyone became a part of everyone else's life.

The growth of a civil society is explored in the TV series *Deadwood,* and other aspects of it in the films *High Noon* and *The Postman.*

Examples in History and Current Events
No matter what period or where your story takes place, you can use some of these real-world examples of civil societies in their various stages, from the glorious to the failed.

Real people involved in these times and places can become characters. The situations can inspire and/or frame the plot and background for the development of your story.

In Ancient Times
- Athens – the city-state that founded democracy and thrived for hundreds and hundreds of years
- Rome - went from a small backwater (supposedly) founded by refuges from the Trojan War to a powerful far-reaching Empire
- Crete – thought to have been matriarchal at one time, their standard of living was high (with running water and central heat), and they carried on trade across the Mediterranean

- Tenochtitlan – the Aztec city-state, also highly developed with aqueducts, steam baths, and astronomical observatories whose calculations remained unrivaled until the early 20th century
- Babylon – a city-state in Mesopotamia (the Middle East). It started as a small town, became a "holy city", was the seat of the early law-giver Hammurabi, went into decline, then came back again, and again. It's a colourful example of the rise and fall of a civil society battered by conquest but continually arising.
- Beijing/Peking – this Chinese city is three thousand years old and has for most of that time been the center for politics and culture for the large empire. More primitive societies have been there as far back as 250,000 years ago, when we upright naked apes weren't quite human yet. Geography contributed to this place's success with protective mountains, major rivers and a varied climate in which civil society could develop.
- Althingi – Iceland's Parliament, the oldest extant in the world, is an excellent example of civil society
- Bedouin – an ancient nomadic people whose mores of hospitality and justice helped them survive the harsh desert landscapes of the Arabian peninsula
- the Iroquois Nation was made up of the indigenous peoples of NE America and was the model for the founding of American government
- tribes of Anasazi populated the American southwest until they disappeared; some think because of climate change
- Angkor's civil society remains impressive in its ruins throughout Cambodia

See more in Will and Ariel Durant's classic world historical series *The Story of Civilization*.

In Current Times
- Bedouin – continuing to this day, they still have a working civil society. They were instrumental in the Allied defeat of Turkey in World War I. [See *Lawrence of Arabia* to see it in action.] However, the Bedouin are citizens of the desert not

of the city, and this was a problem for Lawrence and Sherif Ali. After winning the battle for Damascus, the desert nomads - unfamiliar with the power grids and water systems of a city - had to relinquish control to the British.

- The Amish – this isolationist civil society is religion-based and eschews modern conveniences. After having gone into the outside world for a time, teenagers must decide on their own whether to return to the Amish lifestyle. Their belonging is dependent upon free will but the civil society itself is very ordered and traditional. All adult members contribute to the whole and are expected to follow the rules.
- Hong Kong and Macao - former city-states ruled respectively by the British and the Portuguese, they're now ruled by mainland China but still have different laws and are currently positioning themselves for more freedoms.
- Singapore – their civil society was planned and enforced and has created a very prosperous city-state with a high quality of life.
- The Spanish town of Marinaleda is a thriving example of a civil society based on socialist principles.
- On a larger scale the coming together of local communities results in nationalism. The history of the Vikings is one of roaming intruders who eventually settled and developed civil societies in city states and continued on to build the powerful socialist nation states that exist today in Scandinavia. Responsibility is shared by all (including paying taxes) and all benefit from a civil society that offers some of the highest standards of living on the planet as well as the highest 'happiness' quotient.
- Kibbutzes and communes are specifically designed civil societies based on a defined and exclusive set of values and actions.
- The Caribbean island country of Grenada's motto is: "Ever conscious of God We Aspire, Build and Advance as One People".

In the Future

- The **Hong Kong Jockey Club** describes its mission and actions thusly on its website: The range and diversity of recipient projects and programmes reflect the Club's objective which is to add value where it will provide the greatest benefit to society as a whole. The Club serves six principal areas of civic and social need: promoting a healthy living; lending a hand and volunteering; creating possibilities; developing sports, fun and games; cultivating arts and culture; and preserving and creating jobs. Working with Government and non-profit agencies, the Club aims to improve the quality of life of the people of Hong Kong and immediate relief to those most in need. In addition to this ongoing work, the Club proactively identifies and generates projects that anticipate future community and social needs.
- **Benefit Corporation** This new paradigm is an excellent example of corporations taking responsibility for their impact on their workers, their communities, and the world. As the B Corp website explains, "B Corps create higher quality jobs and improve the quality of life in our communities. And, as the movement grows, it has become an increasingly powerful agent of change. We are passing laws. We are driving capital."
- **Birth2Work** This organization is dedicated to "Igniting Community Leadership" and "Helping Communities Develop Capable People From Birth to Work". They work with community stakeholders to bring government, community, business, the media, healthcare, education and retired professionals together with families and children in a holistic approach to help create and sustain a civil society beneficial to all. Check out their resource center, radio show, and opportunities for engagement.
- Marinaleda is a small town of 2,700 people in Spain. It is a non-capitalist society that exhibits a love of community, personal responsibility, and individual involvement. Its form is far different from most other societies in that it is a bottom-up alternative of how a civil society can be consciously created. As they explain on their website, "By Social Democracy we understand unlimited access to all

forms of well-being for the whole population of our village. We have always thought that liberty without equality is nothing, and that democracy without real well-being for real people is an empty word and a way of deceiving people, making them believe they are part of a project when in fact they are not needed at all."

- Dystopian societies in various states of dissolution or of growth towards positive civil societies can be seen in *Under the Dome, Mad Max, The Postman,* and *Waterworld.*
- Various new technologies designed to actually control society are portrayed in *Blade Runner, The Fifth Element, Brave New World, Soylent Green* and *Minority Report.*
- Off-world experiences that bring diverse groups of people together in social order for self-protection, commerce, and learning about each other are evidenced in *Babylon 5, Battlestar Galactica,* and *Deep Space 9.*
- And don't forget *Outland – High Noon* in space.
- In Nigeria the radio soap *Story* aims to improve awareness among Nigerians of their rights and responsibilities as citizens and ways to hold government to account.
- In the realm of today's cyber-communities this only works when personal responsibility and involvement support and contribute to all the members of the group.
- On the darker side, though we might not like the motives, the methods, or the results, a dictatorship or a drug cartel uses the tools of a civil society, enforcing individuals to work for the cause of the group. This opens up the discussion of "When evil prevails" as in the film *Chinatown,* or in Mussolini's Fascist Italy where the trains ran on time, but the price for that orderliness was astonishingly high.
- *Inter-Stellar.* In that film, climate change is forcing humans off the earth to look for a new home. Civil society is in a shambles and will need to be re-created in each new place.

"Today, as in every generation, we stand at a crossroads. Our highest task is educating young people to do more than just pull levers. We must train them in the art of critical thinking and imbue them with a love of learning," Powers said. "A university education is predicated on the notion that after the experience, citizens would not only know more, but care more, and make the journey from knowing to caring to acting."

University of Texas President William Powers, Jr.
September 29, 2011

DEVOLUTION
In the above we were exploring more beneficial, higher-turn-of-the-spiral civil societies.

However, we as media creators know that drama is stronger when things don't work right. As man and/or nature devolve, more people are going to be adversely affected.

Here we'll explore problems both manmade and not, from corruption to natural disasters. The movie *Live Free or Die Hard* is an excellent example of an attack on infrastructures and how the breakdown would manifest locally. Cyber attacks and technology failures also led to the Butlerian Jihad against computers in Frank Herbert's *Dune* series. These situations greatly destabilize, disrupt and sometimes completely destroy a civil society.

The TV series *Treme,* set in New Orleans right after Katrina, shows how their fragile compact of civil society was dissolved by the hurricane. There was governmental mis-handling both before and after, from a corrupt local police force to faulty civil engineering of levees, followed by an often ineffectual FEMA. It was America's costliest natural disaster and one of the five deadliest hurricanes in U.S. history.

War typically results in the devolution of civil society, particularly for the losers. Current day ISIS in the Middle East is using rape, kidnapping, and beheadings to break down family and community structures in many areas of Syria. The same also applies with the Boko Haram in parts of sub-Saharan Africa. They are specific powerful war weapons designed especially to undermine the families and local cultures for generations to come.

The Collapse of Western Civilization by Naomi Oreskes and Erik M. Conway is set in 2399. In this fictionalization, a Chinese historian chronicles the decline and fall of the West brought on by climatic changes due to natural cycles and exacerbated by damages from fossil fuels, plus the market failure of unchecked capitalism – all of which drastically affected all parts of any civil society.

All economic and environmental disasters, like all politics, are local.

1. Other destabilizing influences on the social norms can occur when good people do nothing, as in *Batman Begins* or when Frank Miller and his gang are coming to town but no one will back the Sheriff at the showdown in *High Noon*. The rejection of social responsibilities will always have a deleterious affect on local societies. Respect and mutual support are always essential in the development of a strong local community.

    Unfortunately American civil society of the 2000s is more conspicuous by its absence than its presence: politics, screaming talking heads, road rage, queue flare-ups, obnoxious cell-phone users, cattle-car airline travel, etc.

2. Unregulated, unbalanced situations such as greed, graft and corruption, poisoned water or food supplies, and crumbling infrastructure can impact everyone in that community and things too quickly can become quite uncivil. Stories such as *Erin Brokovich, Silkwood,*

Promised Land, *Mulholland Falls*, and *Chinatown* portray these situations.

At the beginning of the Industrial Revolution the British Crown closed down many millennia-old Commons of the British villages, where everyone had previously been able to graze their herds and farm the land, keeping the bounty of their labour for their own use. As a result of these closings, people had to work for someone else to get their food rather than grow it themselves and many were forced off the land and into the factories as menial workers.

The American consumer culture has contributed to the fracturing of civil society such that more products are sold because there are more households needing cars, towels, refrigerators, TVs, etc.

Extraction capitalism is when big companies or empires come in and extract, often by force, bribery and corruption the natural resources of the lands. This often forces long-standing civil societies back into the chaotic and often damaging boom town phase such as the timber industry in Indonesia, cobalt mining in Africa, and oil shale fracking throughout North America.

In *Avatar*, discovery and mining of Unobtainium pulled the native N'avi civil society down into Boom Town mode as hundreds of off-worlders came in to take advantage of the natural resources on Pandora, at the expense of the lifestyles and increasingly the lives of the N'avi.

3. Beyond man's foibles and fallibilities that might lead to a degeneration in civil society, nature can also have a hand in the same process. Floods, forest fires, landslides, and dust storms have all been in our news as of late. These are just the beginnings of incidents that may well create a forced change in civil society, as such occurrences have in the past. Earthquakes, volcanoes, hurricanes, droughts, and tsunamis all have major impacts on human communities. The surface of the earth bears many scars of

meteor and asteroid strikes, one of which wiped out the dinosaurs 65 million years ago. Chances are there will be more and if humans are still on the planet, we're likely to be severely affected.

Climate change carries with it the same potential for destruction, and we are already seeing ocean level rises that will soon cause mass migrations from shorelines and islands around the world. Droughts, floods, extreme cold, heat waves, super-storms...they're all happening now and all affect both local and extended systems of civil societies.

And then there are plagues and diseases which disrupt communities and undermine civil society as people's instinctive survival response takes over. In the 1300s the Black Death wiped out 30-60% of the European populace and brought on major upheavals in social, religious, and political arenas. Story-telling still flourished, as evidenced by Giovanni Boccaccio's book *The Decameron*, a series of 100 novellas about love, sex, tragedy and comedy set in Italy during the Black Plague. Swedish director Ingmar Bergman made *The Seventh Seal*, a film about a man playing chess with Death during that Plague.

In 1918 there were more casualties from the Spanish Flu pandemic than battlefield deaths in all four years of World War I. Stories in the Bible dramatically recount ten plagues around the exodus of the Hebrews from Egypt, and the prophesied seven plagues of the Book of Revelation. You can also include AIDS and the Ebola outbreaks as well as swine flu, bird flu, and other diseases in story arcs, as with *Outbreak, Philadelphia,* and *Angels in America*.

Regardless of man's sense of responsibility to his community these naturally occurring disasters can overwhelm the ability to respond quickly. Fortunately there are organizations that specialize in disaster preparedness and response, but it is still highly traumatic and offers you a very dramatic setting for a story.

4. The extreme foreigner, the other-worldly, the off-worldly, and the blood-thirsty can have strong effects on a civil society. These can include zombies, vampires, werewolves, and aliens such as from the far ends of the universe in search of the tesseract or resources, human forms to inhabit or to eat, or human "precious bodily fluids". Examples include *World War Z, Fire in the Sky, Close Encounters of the Third Kind, Shaun of the Dead, Them, Invaders from Mars, Mars Attacks, Independence Day, Battle of Los Angeles....* To the detriment of law and order, most people panic as the survival instinct kicks in and it's everyone-for-themselves. There's very little civility and caring for others; those who do offer help and sanity are the heroes of these kinds of stories.

In the movies in which Frankenstein appears, his presence destabilizes the local populace to riot and destruction. They storm the castle with pitchforks and torches. This motivation is brought about strictly by fear. The same concept applies to vampires, zombies, werewolves, and aliens in that fear and uncertainty degrades the civil cohesiveness of the community. There's a great *Twilight Zone* episode about aliens using fear to whip up hysteria, causing small town residents to kill each other – "The Monsters are due on Maple Street".

Werewolves and vampires have a parasitic relationship with humans, in that they depend on live humans for their own lives. With zombies and evil aliens [not like *ET* and *Starman*], it's about total annihilation. This distinction will make a difference in how you tell your story.

Galaxy Quest is an excellent example of good aliens trying to hang onto their civil society and their lives and bad aliens trying to destroy them, all within the same story. Plus it's lots of fun.

5. Breakdown of the family.

> *The golf links lie so near the mill*
> *That almost every day*
> *The laboring children can look out*
> *And watch the men at Play.*

> Sarah Norcliffe Cleghorn
> 1876-1959 *Quartrain* [1915]

a. The sociological effects of family can be altered by the agendas of the ruling class. Decisions by others can lead to the breakdown of families, such as with China's one-child law. The breakdown was that everyone wanted a boy and it got to the point where they had to kidnap young girls from distant regions so that a young man could have a wife, because there were so few local girls. Conquerors often force people to emigrate, breaking family ties and ties with the land. They also often impregnate the local females and stir up the gene pool. Sometimes the progeny is accepted, sometimes they are outcast, but it always affects local civil society.

b. The Industrial Revolution (beginning in 1760) drew people from rural areas to the cities to work in factories, shifting family dynamics. In 1950s America, the introduction of the interstate system created the suburbs with single family homes, further separating family units (e.g. grandparents from the children and grandchildren; aunts, uncles and cousins from their kin). 1950s marketing, ala the TV series *Mad Men* and the film *The Man in the Gray Flannel Suit*, learned how to sell products to these smaller units and further fracture these family structures. The more separated family units there are, the more cars, toasters, and stuff you call sell. Historically there have been vertical families (up and down the family tree you're born into) but with its breakup we see more lateral families (the ones you create by choice). Many of these new families are collaborative with much sharing of resources, thus cutting down on consumerism.

c. In the Industrial Revolution children were often forced to work hours opposite those of their parents so the factories could run day and night. In today's Information Revolution (computer-cyber-digital), children are actually forging the way with the new technologies because they are inherently better at it than older people, who have to adapt and retrain their approach to almost everything. Younger people never have to adapt as it is all they have ever known. They may still reside in the same home but they live in a totally different world, most of it online and physically alone. This breaks the cycle in the family where father and mother lead the way. Now multi-billion dollar companies are bought and sold every day by people who may not have finished school, or who did not go to college, and may have made their first billion before they turned twenty. This is a significant shift in the family which also leads to a shift in the dynamics of civil society. Emotional investment in your community is diminished when technology edges out personal responsibility.

d. Today's drive by gay and lesbian couples to marry and have children can result in a stronger civil society. Yet some members of heterosexual society seem unwilling accept this change, even in the face of a divorce rate well over fifty percent. The TV series *Modern Family* is a popular award-winning portrayal of different unit dynamics – including gay dads – within an extended family. The award-winning series *Transparent* is breaking new ground in entertaining ways.

Examples in Media

THE AMERICAN EXPERIMENT

Rugged Individualism
   Jeremiah Johnson   *Quigley Down Under*
   Pale Rider   *High Plains Drifter*
   Robinson Crusoe and the 12th century character
   Hayy Ibn Yaqzan   *Australia*
   Treasure of the Sierra Madre

Boom Towns
   Deadwood   *Hell on Wheels*
   Silverado   *Tombstone*

   Wyatt Earp – the actual person and what he did

Civil Society
   In *Sergeant York,* Walter Brennan owns the
   local store. He reads, owns the first car, and gets
   the first telephone. He's the local preacher and
   becomes the first mayor. Whoever needs
   something comes to him. It's why the general
   store owners had chess and checker games,
   chairs, benches, sometimes free snacks. It was
   an informal town hall where the business –
   public and private – of the community was
   discussed and molded over coffee, tea, or liquor.
   Civil society begins and is sustained in the
   gathering place of the citizens: the town square,
   the commons, around the campfire.

In and Out. Small town high school teacher Kevin Kline doesn't realize he's gay until he's outted by a former student trying to honor him. On the verge of marriage, he's exceptionally confused and the town is all aflutter about the news. The high school principle wants to fire him. Eventually Kevin realizes he is gay. His fiancé is devastated, but the student body, his family, and the whole town stands with him for a happy ending.

In his *Mars* trilogy books, Kim Stanley Robinson portrays the creation, sustaining, and sometimes dissolution of different kinds of civil systems. Colonists on Mars form varied societies: nomadic, matriarchal, industrial- and consumer-centered, self-sustaining ecologically centered, and blends of the above.

The 1960s TV series *The Jetsons* idealized how technology would improve civil society. But...where's my flying car?!

It's a Wonderful Life. An angel shows an individual on the verge of suicide how his contributions to civil society are vital to the well-being of his community. He shows George Bailey [Jimmy Stewart] what would have happened had he not stayed in Bedford Falls and been who he was and done what he did. The message is about the value of individuals like George Bailey who sacrifice their personal dreams for the good of the community; without him the town would wither and die.

In Ancient Times
    Ben Hur   *The Ten Commandments*
    Stargate
    The Shires in *Lord of the Rings* and *The Hobbit*

In Current Times
>*Utopia* – Fox reality series (2014)
>*Greater Tuna* - the plays
>British village mysteries: *Agatha Christie, Midsomer Murders, Miss Bradley Mysteries*
>*Friday Night Lights*   *Power of One*
>*Our Town* – Thornton Wilder play
>*Little Abner* - stage play and comics
>*It Takes a Village* - Hilary Clinton's book
>*Gilmore Girls* – This series set in a small New England town has humourous town hall meetings with wacky personalities who are usually trying to make the community a better place, but their disparate agendas cause problems.

In the Future
>*Battlestar Galactica*   *Babylon 5*
>*Deep Space Nine*

Devolution
War, Genocide, Murderous Military Dictatorships
>*Mad Max, Road Warrior, Beyond Thunderdome* - In this trilogy the first movie is about the breaking up of civil society, the second is about total chaos and survival, and the third is about beginning to rebuild civil society, albeit rough and weird.
>*Apocalypse Now Redux* [the French plantation family]
>*Hotel Rwanda*
>In *The Postman*, Kevin Costner creates a pony express mail service to help rebuild a civil society after an apocalypse.
>Rick's bar in *Casablanca* is a family and a civil society, and he insists upon everyone being civil.

Social Responsibility [the lack thereof]

175

In *High Noon* and *Bad Day at Blackrock* the locals were afraid to bond up and go against the bad guys, to act as a civil society and do the right thing as a group. *Outland* (1981) is *High Noon* in space.
Joel Schumacher's 1993 *Falling Down*
Les Miserables
Lord of the Flies – William Golding 1954

Greed, Graft, and Corruption
Hunger Games
Chinatown and *The Two Jakes* dramatize how the auto-oil-tire giants ruled to the destruction of existing and future mass transit systems in Los Angeles.

In *Jaws*, the greedy town fathers put financial gains against the safety of the citizens. Another example is *A Touch of Evil*.

Whenever you have any large industry attempting to supplant the desires of the local citizenry for its own benefit you have a situation ripe for drama, often in a David vs. Goliath kind of way. *Silkwood, Erin Brokovich, Promised Land, The Englishman Who Went Up a Hill and Came Down a Mountain, Dallas Buyers Club, The Constant Gardner*

Nature
Deep Impact & *Armageddon* are nearly identical: all of humanity is in danger and the heroes are out there to save the world.
Grapes of Wrath
Dante's Peak

Aliens
Attack of the Body Snatchers   *Prometheus*
Mars Attacks   *Cowboys & Aliens*

Breakdown of the Family
> *Downton Abbey* is one family's experience of civil society undergoing change from a rigidly stratified class system to a more free-flowing one and the problems that ensue.
> *Warriors* – in Walter Hill's 1979 film the gangs are families
> Wyatt Earp and family
> Any Tennessee Williams play
> *North & South*   *Dune*

Examples in Music
"Do Not Forsake Me, Oh My Darling" – Tex Ritter for *High Noon*
"I was born in a small town" – John Cougar Mellenkamp
"My Hometown" – Bruce Springsteen
 "Death to My Hometown" - Bruce Springsteen

Symbols
Groups of people
Beehive
Knots
Joined hands
Town meeting
Empty streets
An individual steps up, the group follows their lead

Key Element – Shining Moment
Individuals coming together as a group to create order out of chaos.

The crowd scene in every *Frankenstein* movie where the townspeople come together with torches and pitchforks to fight the local evil.

In *To Kill a Mockingbird,* see the scene where Scout, attorney Atticus Finch's little girl, innocently shames the white men intent on lynching a black man.

An individual stepping to the front and taking a leadership role, usually entailing self-sacrifice for the greater good. In *The Avengers* there's a scene in Stutgard where Loki orders a crowd of citizens to kneel before him. An old German man stands up and says, "Not to men like you." Loki brags, "There are no men like me." The old man bravely counters, "There are always men like you."

In Your Stories
This type of love is a good backdrop to a storyline about a time and place like a city, or a young town, or a developing community. Your protagonist and antagonist work against this backdrop, often because it's what they are fighting for or over, as in *High Noon* and *Deadwood.*

The opportunity for drama exists in both the building up and in the breaking down of a civil society. In the former your protagonist goes up against a status quo, rivals, inertia.

In the latter, your heroine must fight for survival of self and others in the community against dangers personal, impersonal, and supra-personal.

Most apocalyptic and post-apocalyptic stories are played out against the unraveling of civil society.

Written Descriptions
Start your story with a representation of the people in that community. The popular British detective series *Midsomer Murders*, for instance, often begins with the camera following the milkman or postman or village gossip on her bicycle around the charming English village and introducing the local characters, some of whom will soon be dead, and some one or more who'll be revealed as the murderer.

In terms mythologist Joseph Campbell used to describe the Hero's Journey, it's about setting up the "ordinary world" from which the hero will have to depart.

When the situation is good things are bright, the streets are clean and well-lighted, you depict your people as friendly and helpful, demonstrating their civic pride and being responsible for their civic duty. Examples are Mara Purl's *Milford-Haven* book series, *Eureka, In and Out, Witness, Wizard of Loneliness,* and *Gilmore Girls.*

Using specific words such as "community, group, village, society, together, as one, unified, etc." in description or dialogue can help anchor the positive concept of civil society.

On the negative side towns are often depicted at night, in rain, dark and broken, with cold and huddled masses, barred windows, gates, isolated heroes, and corrupt special interest groups. They show more of the dark underbelly of society rather than the mutually supportive "bright sunshiny day".

Film noir builds its power upon the lone hero who works against a background of a corrupt community. Examples are Raymond Chandler's books and David Lynch's movies, Philip K. Dick novels and movies made from them: *Blade Runner, Total Recall* and *Minority Report.*

Cinematic Techniques
As a reminder that the story is about or is set against the background of a community you can use a shot wide enough to include several or many other people...even a town's worth. You see this used a lot in the TV series *Eureka*. In *Jaws* you see bits and pieces of the town as people excitedly talk about the problem of the killer shark. That and all the seersucker tells you it's an East Coast little town.

Show people being drawn to a person or a place as if they are nails drawn to a magnet. This is often best done with an overhead shot. Start close on the special place or person then pull back and up until you have the screen filled with the action of people streaming together.

The antithesis of that is when you show the same streets empty and it's just the protagonist alone fighting evil for the town which is not supporting him, as in *High Noon*.

The domain shot is a different type of environmental shot; it is a character's point of view of the realm in which the story takes place. In *Deadwood* Ian McShane stands on the second floor balcony of his bar and hotel and looks up and down the main street and beyond at Deadwood, his domain. His rival Powers Booth does the same thing from the second story balcony of his whorehouse and we get that both men are fighting for dominance over the same domain.

Other examples of a domain shot are Batman standing atop a precipice looking out over Gotham, Superman flying over the city, Tony Stark looking out over his domain from the top floor of the Stark Building, and in a much larger scope, in *Thor* the guardian of the Bifrost who sees everyone in the universe.

Conclusion
In this chapter we have seen that the love of community is essential to a healthy civil society.

Civil society in action doesn't have to be a democracy like America, it can be social democracies as in Europe, it can be village groups, clans, tribes, neighborhoods in big cities, rural communities, etc. It's about individuals accepting personal responsibility and engaging with the group to bring about the greater good for the greater number.

Love of community can be the plot or a sub-plot; it can be the driver of a character's actions or it can be the background against which your story is played.

What about the conflict between those who resist community and those who desire it?

What about civil societies that become corrupted or possibly endangered by nature?

These dynamics further your drama and increase the storytelling possibilities.

"It is possible that the next Buddha will not take the form of an individual. The next Buddha may take the form of a community – a community practicing understanding and loving kindness, a community practicing mindful living. This may be the most important thing we can do for the survival of the earth."

Thich Nhat Hanh

*****
Exercise #1 - Awareness
Name both a utopia and a dystopia from myth, media, or real life and explain why you selected them.

*****
Exercise #2 – Writing
Write a scene about a community overcoming a problem that they had not been able to solve individually.

Write a scene where the community is not working together or supporting each other, such that responsibility falls onto one citizen rather than on them all.

*****
Further Reading
Non-fiction
Birth2Work
Edmund O. Wilson
Jurgen Habermas
Levi Strauss
Michel Foucault
Margaret Mead - especially her work in Samoa

www.nextdoor.com - connecting neighbors for local services, babysitting, watch, etc.

Pericles - 500 BCE Greece

Aftershock: The Next Economy & America's Future - Robert Reich

Cities and the Wealth of Nations – Jane Jacobs

Collapse of Western Civilization – Naomi Oreskes and Erik M. Conway

It Takes a Village – Hilary Clinton

It's Complicated – Danah Boyd

Seven Pillars of Wisdom, The – T.E. Lawrence, of Arabia

Story of Civilization, The – Will & Ariel Durant

Price of Civilization, The: Reawakening American Virtue and Prosperity - Jeremy Sachs

Republic, The - Plato

System, The: Seeking the Soul of Commerce – Rick Stephens & Elane V. Scott

Unsafe at Any Speed – Ralph Nader

Village Effect The: How Face-to-Face Contact Can Make Us Healthier, Happier, and Smarter – Dr. Susan Pinker

Watchman's Rattle, The - Thinking Our Way Out of Extinction – Rebecca D. Costa

Fiction

Agatha Christie

Dune series – Frank Herbert

Mars Trilogy – Kim Stanley Robinson

Midsomer Murders – Caroline Graham

Milford-Haven series – Mara Purl

Snowcrash – Neal Stephenson

Tennessee Williams

To Kill a Mockingbird – Harper Lee

Wizard of Loneliness – John Nichols

Further Viewing

Alien Nation

Babylon 5

Bad Day at Black Rock

Batman Begins

Big Sleep, The

Blast from the Past
Boondock Saints
Chinatown and *The Two Jakes*
Day the Earth Stood Still, The [1951]
District Nine
Elysium
Escape from New York
Farewell, My Lovely
Friday Night Lights
Gattaca
Going Postal
Gotham
Greater Tuna, Texas
In The Heat of the Night
Inspector Morse and *Inspector Lewis*
L.A. Confidential
Lawrence of Arabia
Murder, She Wrote
Operation Dumbo Drop
Untold History of the United States, The – Oliver Stone
Stars Fell on Henrietta
Stand and Deliver
Star Trek Deep Space Nine
Streets of Fire
To Kill a Mockingbird
Transparent
Twin Peaks
Wall-E
Wild Bunch, The

CONCLUSION

We must continue as storytellers to create media that explores the rich panoply of love we humans experience.

Here in Volume One we have looked at many types of love, how to set up and portray various versions of love, how to plot out believable character arcs, and ways to enrich your stories to attract and fulfill the emotions of your readers and viewers.

There will be more. Additional Volumes cover such types of love as zombie love, May-December romances, narcissism (self-love), thrill of the hunt, and many more.

It may truly be that Love is All There Is, but until then we count on our artists to point the way, to shine a light in the darkness, and to show us how to cherish the many chambers of the heart.

MONTY HAYES McMILLAN is a filmmaker, writer, and photographer with over 30 years in the media industry.

He attended film school at the University of Texas in Austin, where he was also an editor on *Carroscolendas*, an Emmy Award winning bi-lingual educational program. After college Monty co-founded Thor Projects, Inc., a media production and promotion company which established the IATSE Film Union Local in Austin.

For the Office of the Governor, Monty was location manager on *Texas Coastal Wildlife,* an environmental film about the fragile balance of industry and nature along Texas's Gulf of Mexico.

After moving to Los Angeles in 1976, McMillan worked as a producer, director, writer, still photographer, production manager, assistant director, and media consultant on features, commercials, TV series, documentaries, industrials, and military films. Monty was assistant director on director Frank Darabont's WOMAN IN THE ROOM, a short film based on a Stephen King story.

Returning to his roots, Monty was location manager on *Waltz Across Texas*, a feature film set in the Texas oil-fields. The job required training with Red Adair Oil Well Fire Control.

Life on the Slope, a documentary on the people who live and work on the North Slope of Alaska, was directed by McMillan. Filming in minus-80˚ temperatures and near total darkness, his locations on America's Arctic coast included oil rigs, the open tundra, and Eskimo townships.

In conjunction with extensive research for *The Rig*, a feature length screenplay set on an offshore oil rig, Monty produced a documentary filmed on Penrod 78, then the largest semi-submersible rig drilling deep in the Gulf of Mexico.

As leader of a Mata-Hari Productions team, Monty helped establish TV-3, Malaysia's first Public Television Network in Kuala Lumpur. His team included experts in television and video directing, editing, camera, art direction, and sound.

Monty was media consultant for *People to People: Heart to Heart,* a peace conference sponsored by the Houston Intertribal Council. Representatives from 25 North American tribes met with indigenous peoples in the Ecuadorian Andes, plains, and jungles.

For *The Dhamazzadhi Bell*, Monty traveled to Burma in the mid-90s, dealing with the ruling generals and religious leaders in conjunction with a project to locate and raise a giant temple bell lost in Rangoon Harbor in the 15th century.

Other research and filming expeditions have taken McMillan to Mexico, the Philippines, and throughout Southeast Asia.

He has met with corporate, military, and government personnel including the U.S. State Department and Embassies both here and abroad, Chinese and other foreign Embassies, NASA/Jet Propulsion Laboratory, the Smithsonian Air and Space Museum, Pan American Airlines, McDonnell Douglas, provincial governors, and tribal chieftains.

McMillan was West Coast director for AUSA's *America's Army* TV series. He was director-writer for the U.S. Army Signal Command briefing video and also worked on a recruitment film for the Marines. Monty was research analyst on *Friend and/or Foe: The New Security Challenge* for the American Institute of Aeronautics and Astronautics, and on *Projecting Power From the Sea* for the Navy League and Hughes Aircraft. He attended both the Army War College and Air War College National Security Forums and is a life member of the Navy League.

Monty was media consultant for the China Exploration and Research Society, a Donor Member of the Los Angeles World Affairs Council, a certified member of the Community Emergency Response Team in both Los Angeles and Austin Texas, and was listed in *Who's Who in America* - Millennium Edition.

*****

mythworks@sbcglobal.net
www.mythworks.net
www.mythicchallenges.com
www.alphababeacademy.com

PAMELA JAYE SMITH is a mythologist, author, international consultant/speaker, and award-winning producer/director with over thirty years experience in features, TV, commercials, documentaries, corporate and military films, music videos, and web series.

Smith is the author of *THE POWER OF THE DARK SIDE, INNER DRIVES, SYMBOLS-IMAGES-CODES, BEYOND THE HERO'S JOURNEY,* and *PETRA VOLARE.* She writes articles for ScriptMag, the Writers Store, OpEdNews, and many other publications.

Pamela has appeared as a mythology expert on Fox's *Ice Age: Continental Drift* Special Features, was the on-camera spokesperson for Microsoft's *Age of Mythology* video game, and the *Forbidden Secrets* TV series.

Clients and credits include Disney, Paramount, Universal, RAI-TV Rome, Romance Writers of America, UCLA, USC Film School, American Film Institute, Natl. Film Institute of Denmark, Thot Fiction Marseille France, Pepperdine University, Natl. Assoc. of Broadcasters, The Studio Film Actors Training for German and other European actors, and various festivals and story conferences including the LA Webfest and Marseille Webfest. Others include the American Assoc. of University Women, Junior ROTC, General Motors, Boeing, Hyundai, Hughes Space & Communications, the FBI, and the U.S. Army.
Pamela was a story and design consultant on two Wes Craven films – *Wes Craven's New Nightmare* and *Vampire in Brooklyn.*

The Last Tiger Expedition sought a lost WWII American pilot, Pamela's uncle, whose plane went down in the Himalayas.

Working with NASA/JPL, the Smithsonian, and Pan Am, the project took her and Monty McMillan throughout the US, Hong Kong, Singapore, Malaysia, and Thailand. The plane was found, but not her uncle. Chinese and American government collaboration premiered a museum exhibit at the George Bush Library at Texas A&M and also in Kunming, China, as well as producing a film and a book.

Ms. Smith serves on the Entertainment Industries Council think tank, a Boeing think tank on Workforce Development & Education, and served on the U.S. Army's Advanced Warfighting Working Group at Fort Knox. She attended both Army War College and Air War College National Security Forums and took post-graduate courses in Intelligence at American Military University. Pamela holds a BA in English, Latin, and Film from the University of Texas at Austin. After 8 years formal study in Comparative Mysticism, Pamela is a certified teacher of the Mystery Schools.

Founder of MYTHWORKS – "Applied Mythology for a more Powerful Reality", she coaches writers, does writing-for-hire, and offers consultations on Mythic Tools for individuals and organizations. Pamela is co-founder of the Alpha Babe Academy.

During the 1990s Pamela served on the U.S. Army's Advanced Warfighting Working Group at Fort Knox, consulting on the Warrior Spirit, Leadership, Ethics and Values. She attended Army War College and the Air Force's Air War College. Her production company wrote and designed the 2000 Command Briefing CD for the U.S. Army Signal Command. Pamela was field producer on episodes of "America's Army" TV series. She has driven an M1A1 Tank – for real, and flown fighter jets – in simulators.

Mythic Challenges – "Create Stories that Change the World" brings the story tools of Mythic Themes, Archetypes, and Symbols to media makers addressing the 15 Global Challenges as identified by the Millennium Project and the United Nations. Pamela is co-founder and teacher; the pilot program included students in Los Angeles and Afghanistan and a number of student pieces have won recognition and awards.

Smith served as past president, LA Chapter, of the Pan Pacific SE Asia Women's Assoc., Media Consultant for China Exploration and Research Society, trained for the Community Emergency Response Team, and was listed in the Millennium Edition of *Who's Who in the World*. Pamela is a 3rd degree Master Mason and has served as an officer in a co-ed Lodge with international affiliations.

Various projects have taken Smith to the Arctic, the Andes, SE Asia, Europe, and New Zealand. She has filmed on the largest off-shore oil rig in the Gulf of Mexico, slept in grass huts and eaten guinea pig under Ecuador's highest volcano, caught her own sushi in the Leyte Gulf, and rappelled into the jungles of Mindanao searching for WWII Japanese gold.

Pamela is an avid reader, drives classic cars, and enjoys opera. A dilettante approach to sports has included surfing, skiing, snorkeling, flying, go-cart & auto racing, and driving an off-shore oil rig and an Army tank -- both under close supervision.

****

pjs@pamelajayesmith.com
www.mythworks.net
www.mythicchallenges.com
www.alphababeacademy.com

More Mythic Tools™ to help you improve
your creativity and your craft —

Books

BEYOND THE HERO'S JOURNEY
Other Powerful Mythic Themes

INNER DRIVES
How to Write and Create Characters
Using the Eight Classic Centers of Motivation

PITCHING TIPS FROM ANCIENT AUTHORS

THE POWER OF THE DARK SIDE
Creating Great Villains & Dangerous Situations

SYMBOLS.IMAGES.CODES
Secret Language of Meaning in Media

Books available from MYTHWORKS, Michael Wiese
Productions www.mwp.com, The Writers Store
www.writersstore.com, Amazon, Barnes & Noble, and your
local bookstore.

CDs/Downloads

ALPHA BABES, ARCHEPATHS, BEYOND THE HERO'S JOURNEY, CREATING OUR NEXT MYTHS, CREATIVE CYCLES, WARRIOR WAY FOR FILMMAKERS, and more

Products available from MYTHWORKS and The Writers Store
www.writersstore.com

Consultations

Pamela Jaye Smith - Story Consultations, Writing, Coaching, Speaker, Teacher, Panelist, Workshop Leader

Monty Hayes McMillan - Writing, Directing, Production Consultant, Lighting Designer, Photographer

MYTHWORKS
pjs@pamelajayesmith.com
www.pamelajayesmith.com
www.mythworks.net
www.mythicchallenges.com
www.alphababeacademy.com